Math Practice: Grades 5–6

Table of Contents

© 2009, Carson-Dellosa Publishing Company, Inc., Greensboro, North Carolina 27425. The purchase o̶̶̶̶̶̶̶̶̶ ̶̶̶̶̶ ̶̶̶uyer
to reproduce worksheets and activities for classroom use only—not for commercial resale. Reproduction of these materials for an
entire school or district is prohibited. No part of this book may be reproduced (except as noted above), stored in a retrieval system,
or transmitted in any form or by any means (mechanically, electronically, recording, etc.) without the prior written consent of
Carson-Dellosa Publishing Co., Inc.

Printed in the USA • All rights reserved.

ISBN 978-1-60418-272-9
03-126131151

Ready-to-Use Ideas and Activities

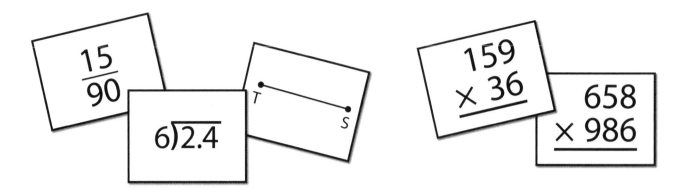

The only way that students will truly be able to manipulate numbers and have access to higher-level math concepts is to learn the basic facts and understand fundamental concepts, such as counting, addition, subtraction, multiplication, and division.

The following activities can help reinforce basic skills. These activities include a multisensory approach to helping students understand the concepts being introduced.

- Separate the flash cards provided in the back of this book. Place the "equal" sign, "greater than" sign, and "lesser than" sign flash cards on a flat surface. Then, place two flash cards with equations on the flat surface. Have students use the sign flash cards to show whether the two equations are equal, one equation is greater than the other equation, or one equation is less than the other equation. Repeat with two different equation flash cards.

CD-104322 • © Carson-Dellosa

Ready-to-Use Ideas and Activities

- Use a pair of dice and anything that can act as a three-minute timer (a timer, a stopwatch, a watch with a second hand, etc.), or decide on a certain number of rounds of play. Have each student roll the dice and multiply the numbers on the top faces. Each correct answer is worth one point. The student with the most correct answers after a specific period of time or number of rounds wins. For example, a game may consist of six rounds. The student with the most points after six rounds wins. Alternately, the game can be played with division with remainders.

- As players memorize answers and gain confidence, add additional dice. When using more than two dice, have players state the problem aloud and answer as they go. For example, if the dice show 5, 2, 6, and 4, the player would say, "5 times 2 is 10, and 10 times 6 is 60, and 60 times 4 is 240."

- Create a bingo sheet with five rows and five columns of blank squares. Write *FREE* in the middle square. Give one copy to each student. Write the flash card equations where they can be seen and have students choose 24 of the equations and write them in the empty spaces of their bingo cards in any order. When students have finished writing on their cards, gather the flash cards into a deck. Call out the equations one at a time. Any student who has an equation that you call out should make an X through the equation on their card to cross it out. The student who crosses out five equations in a row first (horizontally, vertically, or diagonally) wins the game by calling out, "Bingo!" Then, have students solve the equations on their bingo cards.

- Play another version of this game by writing answers on the bingo sheet and calling out the equations. To extend the game, continue playing until a student crosses out all of the answers on her bingo sheet.

Adding Multi-Digit Numbers

Total Problems: 24
Problems Correct: _____

Solve each problem. Regroup when necessary.

1. 56
+ 32

2. 125
+ 832

3. 4,287
+ 907

4. 2,703
+ 9,006

5. 21,027
+ 68,509

6. 17
+ 81

7. 687
+ 407

8. 1,287
+ 406

9. 1,551
+ 3,287

10. 32,578
+ 10,781

11. 95
+ 59

12. 531
+ 450

13. 3,572
+ 261

14. 4,692
+ 7,841

15. 54,392
+ 62,158

16. 27
+ 42

17. 501
+ 225

18. 5,983
+ 742

19. 6,031
+ 3,275

20. 35
+ 80

21. 387
+ 122

22. 6,401
+ 578

23. 8,762
+ 5,137

24. 40,226
+ 37,822

CD-104322 • © Carson-Dellosa

Multi-Digit Column Addition

Solve each problem. Regroup when necessary.

Total Problems: **20**
Problems Correct: _____

1.   234
  862
+ 335

2.   1,767
 8,403
+ 2,759

3. 50,251
   339
+   42

4. 67,107
53,001
42,902
+   107

5.   187
 384
+ 416

6. 5,570
4,867
+ 3,210

7. 69,721
 4,065
+   13

8. 5,545
  632
   19
+   45

9. 486
582
+ 23

10. 1,257
4,380
+ 9,621

11. 8,609
  786
+   52

12. 7,840
2,129
  616
+   53

13. 875
934
+ 17

14. 6,357
1,876
+ 5,072

15. 52,103
47,339
+   857

16. 2,531
  682
  550
+   49

17. 416
502
+ 22

18. 1,275
2,654
+ 3,023

19. 78,695
 4,072
+ 3,210

20. 8,749
7,263
  521
+   84

Multi-Digit Column Addition

Solve each problem. Regroup when necessary.

1.   421
     857
      63
      54
   +   7

2. 52,105
   43,785
    6,112
    3,953
   + 4,182

3. 87,152
    5,847
    1,376
     209
     440
   + 328

4. 5,321
     876
     524
     100
   +   76

5. 78,104
   18,905
    5,629
    3,247
   +   432

6. 33,201
    5,784
    7,206
     628
     552
   +   16

7. 1,019
     593
     422
      42
   +   59

8. 27,862
   50,311
   62,109
    5,450
   + 6,219

9. 68,431
   55,095
   18,702
     457
     212
   +   12

10. 8,763
     257
     812
     404
   +   95

11. 18,782
    3,755
    2,262
     187
   +   555

12. 70,152
   39,157
   70,062
     345
     228
   +   12

13. 52,106
   43,785
    6,112
    3,953
   + 4,182

14. 6,501
     430
     822
      95
   +   42

15. 83,164
   22,900
   18,442
    4,963
     527
   +   89

CD-104322 • © Carson-Dellosa

Name _____ Date _____

Subtracting One- and Two-Digit Numbers

Total Problems: **24**
Problems Correct: _____

Solve each problem. Regroup when necessary.

1. 78
    − 6

2. 25
    − 7

3. 21
    − 5

4. 54
    − 45

5. 17
    − 16

6. 56
    − 4

7. 22
    − 8

8. 19
    − 6

9. 62
    − 27

10. 95
    − 67

11. 60
    − 10

12. 68
    − 9

13. 10
    − 3

14. 85
    − 67

15. 62
    − 56

16. 32
    − 9

17. 70
    − 6

18. 71
    − 4

19. 92
    − 18

20. 38
    − 27

21. 48
    − 8

22. 84
    − 7

23. 34
    − 6

24. 29
    − 17

Subtracting Two- and Three-Digit Numbers

Total Problems: **24**
Problems Correct: _____

Solve each problem. Regroup when necessary.

1. 286
  − 57

2. 991
  − 85

3. 875
  − 407

4. 497
  − 322

5. 603
  − 571

6. 382
  − 96

7. 997
  − 61

8. 962
  − 509

9. 625
  − 592

10. 827
  − 694

11. 186
  − 52

12. 863
  − 54

13. 875
  − 445

14. 940
  − 185

15. 307
  − 283

16. 525
  − 63

17. 415
  − 78

18. 786
  − 616

19. 876
  − 652

20. 125
  − 116

21. 400
  − 88

22. 321
  − 39

23. 521
  − 431

24. 785
  − 504

CD-104322 • © Carson-Dellosa

Subtracting Multi-Digit Numbers

Total Problems: **25**
Problems Correct: _____

Solve each problem. Regroup when necessary.

1. 8,907
   −   52

2. 4,301
   − 225

3. 22,107
   − 3,988

4. 86,946
   − 71,807

5. 302,175
   − 68,189

6. 6,217
   −   25

7. 5,681
   − 309

8. 31,257
   − 4,071

9. 47,810
   − 22,516

10. 496,502
   − 10,498

11. 8,357
   −   78

12. 7,662
   − 447

13. 46,689
   − 5,672

14. 25,300
   − 18,704

15. 187,645
   − 53,217

16. 1,358
   −   32

17. 5,432
   − 151

18. 76,571
   − 6,229

19. 6,219
   −   52

20. 8,719
   − 582

21. 52,398
   − 1,028

22. 86,107
   − 83,279

23. 36,875
   − 31,787

24. 63,128
   − 57,281

25. 94,422
   − 5,349

Multiplying One- and Two-Digit Numbers

Solve each problem. Regroup when necessary.

Total Problems:	**30**
Problems Correct:	_____

1. 6
$\times 9$

2. 5
$\times 3$

3. 11
$\times 4$

4. 12
$\times 5$

5. 9
$\times 3$

6. 4
$\times 7$

7. 10
$\times 3$

8. 8
$\times 8$

9. 10
$\times 4$

10. 7
$\times 8$

11. 8
$\times 9$

12. 5
$\times 8$

13. 5
$\times 5$

14. 12
$\times 12$

15. 4
$\times 5$

16. 11
$\times 2$

17. 11
$\times 10$

18. 12
$\times 4$

19. 11
$\times 9$

20. 7
$\times 9$

21. 10
$\times 10$

22. 10
$\times 9$

23. 10
$\times 8$

24. 11
$\times 8$

25. 4
$\times 3$

26. 5
$\times 7$

27. 9
$\times 6$

28. 11
$\times 12$

29. 6
$\times 3$

30. 6
$\times 6$

CD-104322 • © Carson-Dellosa

Multiplying Two-Digit Numbers

Solve each problem. Regroup when necessary.

1. $\begin{array}{r} 27 \\ \times 13 \\ \hline \end{array}$ 2. $\begin{array}{r} 15 \\ \times 47 \\ \hline \end{array}$ 3. $\begin{array}{r} 84 \\ \times 19 \\ \hline \end{array}$ 4. $\begin{array}{r} 58 \\ \times 61 \\ \hline \end{array}$ 5. $\begin{array}{r} 45 \\ \times 62 \\ \hline \end{array}$

6. $\begin{array}{r} 87 \\ \times 93 \\ \hline \end{array}$ 7. $\begin{array}{r} 22 \\ \times 38 \\ \hline \end{array}$ 8. $\begin{array}{r} 82 \\ \times 27 \\ \hline \end{array}$ 9. $\begin{array}{r} 33 \\ \times 51 \\ \hline \end{array}$ 10. $\begin{array}{r} 46 \\ \times 41 \\ \hline \end{array}$

11. $\begin{array}{r} 47 \\ \times 25 \\ \hline \end{array}$ 12. $\begin{array}{r} 24 \\ \times 43 \\ \hline \end{array}$ 13. $\begin{array}{r} 42 \\ \times 51 \\ \hline \end{array}$ 14. $\begin{array}{r} 87 \\ \times 65 \\ \hline \end{array}$ 15. $\begin{array}{r} 48 \\ \times 62 \\ \hline \end{array}$

16. $\begin{array}{r} 68 \\ \times 59 \\ \hline \end{array}$ 17. $\begin{array}{r} 65 \\ \times 92 \\ \hline \end{array}$ 18. $\begin{array}{r} 23 \\ \times 50 \\ \hline \end{array}$ 19. $\begin{array}{r} 83 \\ \times 60 \\ \hline \end{array}$ 20. $\begin{array}{r} 72 \\ \times 57 \\ \hline \end{array}$

Multiplying Multi-Digit Numbers

Total Problems:	24
Problems Correct:	_____

Solve each problem. Regroup when necessary.

1. $\begin{array}{r} 87 \\ \times\ 5 \\ \hline \end{array}$

2. $\begin{array}{r} 72 \\ \times\ 18 \\ \hline \end{array}$

3. $\begin{array}{r} 425 \\ \times\ 15 \\ \hline \end{array}$

4. $\begin{array}{r} 303 \\ \times\ 83 \\ \hline \end{array}$

5. $\begin{array}{r} 187 \\ \times\ 26 \\ \hline \end{array}$

6. $\begin{array}{r} 93 \\ \times\ 6 \\ \hline \end{array}$

7. $\begin{array}{r} 63 \\ \times\ 25 \\ \hline \end{array}$

8. $\begin{array}{r} 313 \\ \times\ 72 \\ \hline \end{array}$

9. $\begin{array}{r} 442 \\ \times\ 81 \\ \hline \end{array}$

10. $\begin{array}{r} 593 \\ \times\ 45 \\ \hline \end{array}$

11. $\begin{array}{r} 84 \\ \times\ 3 \\ \hline \end{array}$

12. $\begin{array}{r} 42 \\ \times\ 28 \\ \hline \end{array}$

13. $\begin{array}{r} 81 \\ \times\ 53 \\ \hline \end{array}$

14. $\begin{array}{r} 872 \\ \times\ 20 \\ \hline \end{array}$

15. $\begin{array}{r} 351 \\ \times\ 67 \\ \hline \end{array}$

16. $\begin{array}{r} 52 \\ \times\ 4 \\ \hline \end{array}$

17. $\begin{array}{r} 75 \\ \times\ 21 \\ \hline \end{array}$

18. $\begin{array}{r} 21 \\ \times\ 10 \\ \hline \end{array}$

19. $\begin{array}{r} 214 \\ \times\ 87 \\ \hline \end{array}$

20. $\begin{array}{r} 109 \\ \times\ 15 \\ \hline \end{array}$

21. $\begin{array}{r} 12 \\ \times\ 9 \\ \hline \end{array}$

22. $\begin{array}{r} 16 \\ \times\ 8 \\ \hline \end{array}$

23. $\begin{array}{r} 87 \\ \times\ 26 \\ \hline \end{array}$

24. $\begin{array}{r} 99 \\ \times\ 21 \\ \hline \end{array}$

CD-104322 • © Carson-Dellosa

Multiplying Multi-Digit Numbers

Total Problems: **20**
Problems Correct: _____

Solve each problem. Regroup when necessary.

1.   918
    $\times$ 55

2.   755
    $\times$ 221

3.   618
    $\times$ 500

4. 1,242
    $\times$ 687

5.   437
    $\times$ 22

6.   832
    $\times$ 106

7.   391
    $\times$ 125

8. 3,861
    $\times$ 392

9.   518
    $\times$ 42

10.   391
    $\times$ 535

11.   482
    $\times$ 663

12. 4,369
    $\times$ 873

13.   925
    $\times$ 54

14.   851
    $\times$ 462

15.   331
    $\times$ 528

16. 7,421
    $\times$ 694

17.   622
    $\times$ 33

18.   795
    $\times$ 787

19.   435
    $\times$ 683

20. 5,872
    $\times$ 515

Division with One-Digit Quotients

Total Problems: **24**
Problems Correct: _____

Solve each problem.

1. $8\overline{)64}$ **2.** $5\overline{)25}$ **3.** $6\overline{)30}$

4. $5\overline{)40}$ **5.** $4\overline{)20}$ **6.** $9\overline{)81}$

7. $8\overline{)24}$ **8.** $7\overline{)77}$ **9.** $8\overline{)32}$

10. $9\overline{)27}$ **11.** $7\overline{)42}$ **12.** $6\overline{)54}$

13. $6\overline{)36}$ **14.** $3\overline{)12}$ **15.** $5\overline{)30}$

16. $8\overline{)56}$ **17.** $8\overline{)16}$ **18.** $5\overline{)35}$

19. $7\overline{)14}$ **20.** $9\overline{)36}$ **21.** $6\overline{)24}$

22. $9\overline{)90}$ **23.** $9\overline{)63}$ **24.** $6\overline{)60}$

CD-104322 • © Carson-Dellosa

Division with One-Digit Quotients

Total Problems:	**20**
Problems Correct:	_____

Solve each problem.

1. $4\overline{)100}$ 2. $2\overline{)132}$ 3. $3\overline{)225}$ 4. $9\overline{)198}$

5. $2\overline{)902}$ 6. $7\overline{)112}$ 7. $6\overline{)510}$ 8. $4\overline{)216}$

9. $6\overline{)426}$ 10. $2\overline{)630}$ 11. $3\overline{)138}$ 12. $9\overline{)369}$

13. $8\overline{)624}$ 14. $6\overline{)396}$ 15. $8\overline{)648}$ 16. $5\overline{)310}$

17. $5\overline{)425}$ 18. $7\overline{)672}$ 19. $3\overline{)864}$ 20. $7\overline{)966}$

Division with Two-Digit Quotients

Total Problems: **20**
Problems Correct: _____

Solve each problem.

1. 22)308

2. 17)306

3. 24)1,200

4. 86)4,730

5. 73)4,453

6. 11)286

7. 33)957

8. 38)1,064

9. 74)3,848

10. 29)1,798

11. 16)832

12. 53)901

13. 45)1,485

14. 91)5,096

15. 82)1,968

16. 41)574

17. 62)744

18. 57)3,591

19. 18)1,296

20. 95)3,990

CD-104322 • © Carson-Dellosa

Division with One- and Two-Digit Quotients and Remainders

Solve each problem.

1. $8\overline{)75}$

2. $24\overline{)107}$

3. $48\overline{)541}$

4. $18\overline{)472}$

5. $22\overline{)514}$

6. $4\overline{)67}$

7. $16\overline{)451}$

8. $62\overline{)754}$

9. $23\overline{)685}$

10. $42\overline{)684}$

11. $6\overline{)68}$

12. $32\overline{)187}$

13. $13\overline{)541}$

14. $46\overline{)931}$

15. $52\overline{)315}$

16. $3\overline{)79}$

17. $51\overline{)823}$

18. $72\overline{)843}$

19. $50\overline{)657}$

20. $37\overline{)562}$

Division with Two- and Three-Digit Quotients and Remainders

Total Problems: **20**
Problems Correct: _____

Solve each problem.

1. $28\overline{)1{,}570}$

2. $36\overline{)4{,}587}$

3. $81\overline{)9{,}758}$

4. $561\overline{)6{,}398}$

5. $122\overline{)6{,}387}$

6. $16\overline{)2{,}154}$

7. $97\overline{)1{,}863}$

8. $19\overline{)3{,}786}$

9. $117\overline{)2{,}573}$

10. $184\overline{)2{,}514}$

11. $47\overline{)5{,}024}$

12. $65\overline{)7{,}641}$

13. $24\overline{)4{,}597}$

14. $264\overline{)5{,}219}$

15. $512\overline{)4{,}287}$

16. $53\overline{)4{,}523}$

17. $72\overline{)8{,}942}$

18. $38\overline{)4{,}264}$

19. $435\overline{)8{,}708}$

20. $371\overline{)6{,}737}$

CD-104322 • © Carson-Dellosa

Name _____ Date _____

Understanding Fractions

Total Problems: **12**
Problems Correct: _____

Write the fraction for each of the following descriptions.

1. four-fifths _____

2. two-thirds _____

3. three-eighths _____

4. Numerator 1, Denominator 10 _____

5. Denominator 7, Numerator 9 _____

6. Numerator 3, Denominator 4 _____

Shade each shape to show the fraction.

7. $\frac{5}{6}$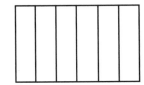

8. $\frac{3}{4}$

9. $\frac{1}{5}$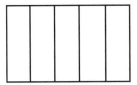

Draw lines to divide each shape. Then, shade each shape to show the fraction.

10. $\frac{1}{2}$

11. $\frac{9}{10}$

12. $\frac{7}{8}$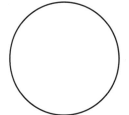

Making Fractions Equivalent

Total Problems: 20
Problems Correct: _____

Make each pair of fractions equivalent.

1. $\dfrac{1}{2} = \dfrac{}{4}$

2. $\dfrac{3}{5} = \dfrac{}{20}$

3. $\dfrac{5}{6} = \dfrac{}{42}$

4. $\dfrac{3}{4} = \dfrac{}{12}$

5. $\dfrac{2}{3} = \dfrac{}{12}$

6. $\dfrac{1}{5} = \dfrac{}{25}$

7. $\dfrac{1}{4} = \dfrac{}{8}$

8. $\dfrac{2}{7} = \dfrac{4}{}$

9. $\dfrac{3}{7} = \dfrac{}{28}$

10. $\dfrac{1}{3} = \dfrac{3}{}$

11. $\dfrac{2}{3} = \dfrac{}{15}$

12. $\dfrac{1}{8} = \dfrac{8}{}$

13. $\dfrac{2}{5} = \dfrac{6}{}$

14. $\dfrac{3}{4} = \dfrac{9}{}$

15. $\dfrac{6}{7} = \dfrac{}{14}$

16. $\dfrac{4}{5} = \dfrac{12}{}$

Fill in the numbers to complete each row, making each fraction equivalent to the first one.

17. $\dfrac{1}{2} = \dfrac{}{6} = \dfrac{4}{} = \dfrac{}{12} = \dfrac{2}{} = \dfrac{}{10}$

18. $\dfrac{2}{3} = \dfrac{}{12} = \dfrac{4}{} = \dfrac{}{15} = \dfrac{6}{} = \dfrac{}{18}$

19. $\dfrac{1}{4} = \dfrac{}{8} = \dfrac{5}{} = \dfrac{}{12} = \dfrac{6}{} = \dfrac{}{16}$

20. $\dfrac{3}{5} = \dfrac{}{25} = \dfrac{9}{} = \dfrac{}{10} = \dfrac{12}{} = \dfrac{}{30}$

CD-104322 • © Carson-Dellosa

Comparing Fractions

Total Problems: **15**
Problems Correct: _____

Write >, <, or = to make each statement true.

1. $\frac{1}{2}$ ◯ $\frac{4}{8}$

2. $\frac{2}{5}$ ◯ $\frac{3}{4}$

3. $\frac{5}{6}$ ◯ $\frac{7}{8}$

4. $\frac{5}{8}$ ◯ $\frac{13}{32}$

5. $\frac{1}{8}$ ◯ $\frac{3}{5}$

6. $\frac{1}{4}$ ◯ $\frac{2}{3}$

7. $\frac{1}{6}$ ◯ $\frac{1}{3}$

8. $\frac{4}{5}$ ◯ $\frac{16}{20}$

9. $\frac{2}{3}$ ◯ $\frac{1}{5}$

10. $\frac{1}{2}$ ◯ $\frac{4}{5}$

11. $\frac{11}{16}$ ◯ $\frac{3}{8}$

12. $\frac{4}{7}$ ◯ $\frac{1}{2}$

Rewrite each series of fractions so that they have like denominators. Order each series from smallest to largest. Then, write each fraction in simplest form.

	Same denominator, smallest to largest	Simplest form
13. $\frac{1}{3}, \frac{3}{4}, \frac{1}{2}$	_____	_____
14. $\frac{5}{6}, \frac{2}{9}, \frac{1}{3}$	_____	_____
15. $\frac{1}{6}, \frac{7}{8}, \frac{3}{4}$	_____	_____

Finding the Greatest Common Factor

Total Problems: **10**
Problems Correct: _____

List the common factors of the numerator and denominator of each fraction. Then, write the greatest common factor (GCF). Divide the numerator and denominator by the GCF and write each fraction in simplest form.

	Fraction	Common Factors	GCF	Simplest Form
1.	$\frac{10}{12}$			
2.	$\frac{18}{27}$			
3.	$\frac{25}{100}$			
4.	$\frac{5}{30}$			
5.	$\frac{12}{30}$			
6.	$\frac{24}{32}$			
7.	$\frac{14}{21}$			
8.	$\frac{8}{40}$			
9.	$\frac{15}{18}$			
10.	$\frac{10}{20}$			

CD-104322 • © Carson-Dellosa

Writing Fractions in Simplest Form

Write each fraction or mixed number in simplest form.

1. $\frac{6}{8} =$

2. $\frac{6}{15} =$

3. $\frac{27}{81} =$

4. $2\frac{24}{30} =$

5. $4\frac{4}{8} =$

6. $\frac{2}{4} =$

7. $\frac{2}{10} =$

8. $\frac{12}{24} =$

9. $3\frac{12}{18} =$

10. $5\frac{10}{15} =$

11. $\frac{15}{18} =$

12. $\frac{20}{40} =$

13. $\frac{10}{15} =$

14. $1\frac{18}{20} =$

15. $3\frac{6}{9} =$

16. $\frac{16}{24} =$

17. $\frac{16}{32} =$

18. $\frac{14}{21} =$

19. $4\frac{3}{24} =$

20. $2\frac{8}{32} =$

21. $\frac{10}{40} =$

22. $\frac{56}{64} =$

23. $3\frac{6}{18} =$

24. $\frac{48}{50} =$

Writing Mixed Numbers as Improper Fractions

Write each mixed number as an improper fraction.

1. $2\dfrac{3}{4} = \dfrac{(\quad \times \quad) +}{4} =$

2. $3\dfrac{1}{3} = \dfrac{(\quad \times \quad) +}{3} =$

3. $2\dfrac{7}{8} = \dfrac{(\quad \times \quad) +}{\quad} =$

4. $7\dfrac{3}{4} = \dfrac{(\quad \times \quad) +}{\quad} =$

5. $1\dfrac{4}{5} = \dfrac{(\quad \times \quad) +}{\quad} =$

6. $4\dfrac{3}{8} = \dfrac{(\quad \times \quad) +}{\quad} =$

7. $1\dfrac{2}{5} = \dfrac{(\quad \times \quad) +}{\quad} =$

8. $4\dfrac{5}{6} = \dfrac{(\quad \times \quad) +}{\quad} =$

9. $2\dfrac{7}{9} = \dfrac{(\quad \times \quad) +}{\quad} =$

10. $5\dfrac{3}{11} = \dfrac{(\quad \times \quad) +}{\quad} =$

CD-104322 • © Carson-Dellosa

Writing Mixed Numbers as Improper Fractions

Write each mixed number as an improper fraction.

1. $2\dfrac{5}{8} =$

2. $3\dfrac{6}{7} =$

3. $8\dfrac{5}{11} =$

4. $8\dfrac{2}{3} =$

5. $4\dfrac{1}{2} =$

6. $8\dfrac{7}{8} =$

7. $3\dfrac{3}{10} =$

8. $2\dfrac{3}{5} =$

9. $6\dfrac{3}{4} =$

10. $2\dfrac{1}{9} =$

11. $4\dfrac{5}{12} =$

12. $5\dfrac{5}{7} =$

Writing Improper Fractions as Mixed Numbers

| Total Problems: | **10** |
| Problems Correct: | _____ |

Write each improper fraction as a mixed number.

1. $\dfrac{15}{8} = 8\overline{)15} =$

2. $\dfrac{25}{13} = 13\overline{)25} =$

3. $\dfrac{54}{7} = 7\overline{)54} =$

4. $\dfrac{29}{5} = \overline{)\quad} =$

5. $\dfrac{85}{22} = \overline{)\quad} =$

6. $\dfrac{10}{4} = \overline{)\quad} =$

7. $\dfrac{62}{8} = \overline{)\quad} =$

8. $\dfrac{34}{10} = \overline{)\quad} =$

9. $\dfrac{43}{16} = \overline{)\quad} =$

10. $\dfrac{33}{7} = \overline{)\quad} =$

CD-104322 • © Carson-Dellosa

Writing Improper Fractions as Mixed Numbers

Write each improper fraction as a mixed number.

Total Problems: **10**
Problems Correct: _____

1. $\dfrac{16}{7} =$

2. $\dfrac{32}{9} =$

3. $\dfrac{37}{12} =$

4. $\dfrac{12}{5} =$

5. $\dfrac{50}{27} =$

6. $\dfrac{10}{4} =$

7. $\dfrac{53}{16} =$

8. $\dfrac{86}{19} =$

9. $\dfrac{14}{13} =$

10. $\dfrac{43}{20} =$

Fractions Review

Total Problems: 25
Problems Correct: _____

Make each pair of fractions equivalent.

1. $\dfrac{3}{4} = \dfrac{}{16}$ **2.** $\dfrac{5}{6} = \dfrac{}{30}$ **3.** $\dfrac{3}{8} = \dfrac{}{32}$

4. $\dfrac{1}{3} = \dfrac{3}{}$ **5.** $\dfrac{5}{12} = \dfrac{25}{}$ **6.** $\dfrac{1}{5} = \dfrac{5}{}$

Write <, >, or = to make each statement true.

7. $3 \bigcirc \dfrac{6}{5}$ **8.** $\dfrac{7}{9} \bigcirc \dfrac{5}{18}$ **9.** $\dfrac{3}{4} \bigcirc \dfrac{2}{3}$

10. $\dfrac{1}{2} \bigcirc \dfrac{1}{3}$ **11.** $\dfrac{12}{24} \bigcirc \dfrac{1}{2}$ **12.** $\dfrac{7}{8} \bigcirc \dfrac{7}{16}$

List the common factors of the numerator and denominator of each fraction. Then, write the GCF. Divide the numerator and denominator by the GCF and write each fraction in simplest form.

	Fraction	Common Factors	GCF	Simplest Form
13.	$\dfrac{12}{24}$			
14.	$\dfrac{21}{28}$			
15.	$\dfrac{16}{32}$			
16.	$\dfrac{45}{54}$			

Write each improper fraction as a mixed number.

17. $\dfrac{25}{15} =$ **18.** $\dfrac{43}{16} =$ **19.** $\dfrac{64}{10} =$

20. $\dfrac{30}{14} =$ **21.** $\dfrac{32}{9} =$ **22.** $\dfrac{10}{8} =$

23. $\dfrac{12}{7} =$ **24.** $\dfrac{16}{12} =$ **25.** $\dfrac{14}{3} =$

   CD-104322 • © Carson-Dellosa

Finding the Least Common Denominator

Total Problems: 12
Problems Correct: _____

Find the least common denominator (LCD) for each pair of fractions.

1. $\frac{3}{5}$, $\frac{3}{7}$ _____

2. $\frac{1}{3}$, $\frac{1}{5}$ _____

3. $\frac{3}{5}$, $\frac{3}{8}$ _____

4. $\frac{1}{3}$, $\frac{3}{4}$ _____

5. $\frac{3}{4}$, $\frac{1}{5}$ _____

6. $\frac{3}{6}$, $\frac{1}{2}$ _____

7. $\frac{1}{4}$, $\frac{3}{8}$ _____

8. $\frac{1}{6}$, $\frac{2}{3}$ _____

9. $\frac{2}{5}$, $\frac{1}{2}$ _____

10. $\frac{5}{6}$, $\frac{3}{5}$ _____

11. $\frac{7}{8}$, $\frac{2}{3}$ _____

12. $\frac{1}{4}$, $\frac{1}{2}$ _____

Adding Fractions with Like Denominators

Total Problems: **15**
Problems Correct: _____

Solve each problem. Write each answer in simplest form.

1. $\dfrac{1}{3} + \dfrac{2}{3} =$

2. $\dfrac{1}{9} + \dfrac{2}{9} =$

3. $\dfrac{3}{6} + \dfrac{2}{6} =$

4. $\dfrac{2}{7} + \dfrac{4}{7} =$

5. $\dfrac{5}{15} + \dfrac{2}{15} =$

6. $\dfrac{1}{4} + \dfrac{3}{4} =$

7. $\dfrac{3}{8} + \dfrac{7}{8} =$

8. $\dfrac{5}{9} + \dfrac{8}{9} =$

9. $\dfrac{7}{12} + \dfrac{2}{12} =$

10. $\dfrac{9}{13} + \dfrac{8}{13} =$

11. $\dfrac{1}{7} + \dfrac{4}{7} =$

12. $\dfrac{7}{10} + \dfrac{1}{10} =$

13. $\dfrac{1}{2} + \dfrac{1}{2} =$

14. $\dfrac{2}{5} + \dfrac{5}{5} =$

15. $\dfrac{4}{12} + \dfrac{3}{12} =$

CD-104322 • © Carson-Dellosa

Adding Fractions with Like Denominators

Solve each problem. Write each answer in simplest form.

Total Problems:	16
Problems Correct:	_____

1. $\frac{4}{9}$
$+ \frac{2}{9}$

2. $\frac{5}{6}$
$+ \frac{1}{6}$

3. $\frac{5}{8}$
$+ \frac{1}{8}$

4. $\frac{4}{5}$
$+ \frac{2}{5}$

5. $\frac{1}{5}$
$+ \frac{2}{5}$

6. $\frac{3}{7}$
$+ \frac{1}{7}$

7. $\frac{1}{3}$
$+ \frac{1}{3}$

8. $\frac{10}{13}$
$+ \frac{11}{13}$

9. $\frac{7}{12}$
$+ \frac{5}{12}$

10. $\frac{2}{15}$
$+ \frac{3}{15}$

11. $\frac{2}{17}$
$+ \frac{4}{17}$

12. $\frac{5}{18}$
$+ \frac{3}{18}$

13. $\frac{7}{10}$
$+ \frac{7}{10}$

14. $\frac{9}{11}$
$+ \frac{6}{11}$

15. $\frac{4}{10}$
$+ \frac{2}{10}$

16. $\frac{1}{2}$
$+ \frac{1}{2}$

Adding Fractions with Unlike Denominators

Total Problems: 15
Problems Correct: _____

Solve each problem. Write each answer in simplest form.

1. $\frac{1}{2} + \frac{2}{5} =$

2. $\frac{1}{6} + \frac{3}{4} =$

3. $\frac{1}{8} + \frac{3}{4} =$

4. $\frac{2}{3} + \frac{3}{4} =$

5. $\frac{5}{12} + \frac{2}{10} =$

6. $\frac{2}{3} + \frac{3}{5} =$

7. $\frac{3}{7} + \frac{1}{3} =$

8. $\frac{1}{9} + \frac{2}{7} =$

9. $\frac{7}{10} + \frac{3}{12} =$

10. $\frac{1}{6} + \frac{3}{5} =$

11. $\frac{1}{4} + \frac{3}{8} =$

12. $\frac{1}{10} + \frac{2}{11} =$

13. $\frac{2}{5} + \frac{1}{3} =$

14. $\frac{2}{7} + \frac{5}{6} =$

15. $\frac{3}{5} + \frac{1}{10} =$

CD-104322 • © Carson-Dellosa

Name _____ Date _____

Adding Fractions with Unlike Denominators

Total Problems: **15**
Problems Correct: _____

Solve each problem. Write each answer in simplest form.

1. $\dfrac{1}{4}$
   $+\ \dfrac{3}{5}$

2. $\dfrac{1}{2}$
   $+\ \dfrac{1}{5}$

3. $\dfrac{4}{5}$
   $+\ \dfrac{2}{3}$

4. $\dfrac{2}{3}$
   $+\ \dfrac{2}{5}$

5. $\dfrac{4}{5}$
   $+\ \dfrac{7}{8}$

6. $\dfrac{3}{4}$
   $+\ \dfrac{1}{3}$

7. $\dfrac{1}{6}$
   $+\ \dfrac{2}{5}$

8. $\dfrac{3}{6}$
   $+\ \dfrac{3}{4}$

9. $\dfrac{1}{4}$
   $+\ \dfrac{2}{3}$

10. $\dfrac{5}{8}$
    $+\ \dfrac{2}{3}$

11. $\dfrac{2}{5}$
    $+\ \dfrac{1}{3}$

12. $\dfrac{1}{3}$
    $+\ \dfrac{5}{7}$

13. $\dfrac{1}{4}$
    $+\ \dfrac{7}{8}$

14. $\dfrac{2}{3}$
    $+\ \dfrac{2}{10}$

15. $\dfrac{1}{3}$
    $+\ \dfrac{2}{6}$

Adding Mixed Numbers with Like Denominators

Total Problems: **12**
Problems Correct: _____

Solve each problem. Write each answer in simplest form.

1. $3\frac{1}{4} + 2\frac{2}{4} =$

2. $5\frac{1}{3} + 2\frac{1}{3} =$

3. $5\frac{8}{9} + 6\frac{2}{9} =$

4. $5\frac{1}{8} + 6\frac{5}{8} =$

5. $5\frac{1}{8} + 2\frac{3}{8} =$

6. $3\frac{1}{6} + 2\frac{1}{6} =$

7. $4\frac{4}{5} + 3\frac{3}{5} =$

8. $4\frac{1}{3} + 5\frac{2}{3} =$

9. $7\frac{2}{9} + 1\frac{5}{9} =$

10. $2\frac{2}{5} + 1\frac{3}{5} =$

11. $2\frac{5}{7} + 3\frac{6}{7} =$

12. $7\frac{5}{6} + 8\frac{4}{6} =$

   CD-104322 • © Carson-Dellosa

Adding Mixed Numbers with Like Denominators

Total Problems:	14
Problems Correct:	_____

Solve each problem. Write each answer in simplest form.

1. $1\frac{6}{8} + 2\frac{4}{8} =$

2. $3\frac{2}{6} + 4\frac{3}{6} =$

3. $5\frac{5}{16} + 3\frac{7}{16} =$

4. $3\frac{1}{4} + 6\frac{1}{4} =$

5. $8\frac{1}{6} + 4\frac{5}{6} =$

6. $3\frac{3}{7} + 4\frac{3}{7} =$

7. $8\frac{5}{6} + 7\frac{5}{6} =$

8. $7\frac{1}{3} + 7\frac{2}{3} =$

9. $\begin{array}{r} 5\frac{3}{8} \\ + 4\frac{1}{8} \\ \hline \end{array}$

10. $\begin{array}{r} 3\frac{9}{10} \\ + 2\frac{7}{10} \\ \hline \end{array}$

11. $\begin{array}{r} 1\frac{5}{12} \\ + 7\frac{11}{12} \\ \hline \end{array}$

12. $\begin{array}{r} 2\frac{7}{9} \\ + 5\frac{4}{9} \\ \hline \end{array}$

13. $\begin{array}{r} 7\frac{4}{5} \\ + 3\frac{1}{5} \\ \hline \end{array}$

14. $\begin{array}{r} 4\frac{2}{3} \\ + 6\frac{2}{3} \\ \hline \end{array}$

Adding Mixed Numbers with Unlike Denominators

Total Problems: **15**
Problems Correct: _____

Solve each problem. Write each answer in simplest form.

1. $4\frac{1}{8} + 5\frac{3}{4} =$

2. $4\frac{7}{8} + 6\frac{1}{4} =$

3. $4\frac{3}{4} + 1\frac{2}{3} =$

4. $4\frac{1}{8} + 5\frac{1}{5} =$

5. $8\frac{3}{4} + 7\frac{3}{16} =$

6. $6\frac{1}{2} + 6\frac{2}{5} =$

7. $8\frac{1}{3} + 2\frac{3}{7} =$

8. $5\frac{1}{8} + 6\frac{2}{5} =$

9. $1\frac{9}{10} + 3\frac{1}{4} =$

10. $2\frac{3}{4} + 3\frac{5}{6} =$

11. $3\frac{1}{9} + 2\frac{1}{3} =$

12. $5\frac{2}{3} + 7\frac{3}{7} =$

13. $2\frac{5}{6} + 3\frac{1}{3} =$

14. $5\frac{1}{2} + 6\frac{2}{7} =$

15. $5\frac{5}{15} + 2\frac{3}{5} =$

Adding Mixed Numbers with Unlike Denominators

Total Problems: 15
Problems Correct: _____

Solve each problem. Write each answer in simplest form.

1. $1\frac{1}{4}$
$+2\frac{5}{6}$

2. $6\frac{7}{12}$
$+8\frac{7}{13}$

3. $5\frac{10}{11}$
$+6\frac{3}{22}$

4. $10\frac{4}{5}$
$+7\frac{1}{8}$

5. $3\frac{3}{4}$
$+6\frac{1}{3}$

6. $9\frac{3}{5}$
$+6\frac{2}{3}$

7. $5\frac{1}{5}$
$+6\frac{2}{4}$

8. $3\frac{2}{3}$
$+4\frac{4}{5}$

9. $8\frac{1}{7}$
$+6\frac{2}{3}$

10. $2\frac{1}{5}$
$+6\frac{1}{4}$

11. $8\frac{5}{6}$
$+3\frac{3}{4}$

12. $5\frac{1}{3}$
$+2\frac{3}{4}$

13. $4\frac{1}{8}$
$+3\frac{1}{2}$

14. $8\frac{9}{10}$
$+4\frac{1}{4}$

15. $8\frac{1}{6}$
$+3\frac{3}{4}$

Subtracting Fractions with Like Denominators

Total Problems: **20**
Problems Correct: _____

Solve each problem. Write each answer in simplest form.

1. $\dfrac{5}{6} - \dfrac{1}{6} =$

2. $\dfrac{3}{4} - \dfrac{1}{4} =$

3. $\dfrac{5}{9} - \dfrac{2}{9} =$

4. $\dfrac{7}{8} - \dfrac{5}{8} =$

5. $\dfrac{3}{7} - \dfrac{2}{7} =$

6. $\dfrac{7}{8} - \dfrac{3}{8} =$

7. $\dfrac{5}{7} - \dfrac{2}{7} =$

8. $\dfrac{5}{8} - \dfrac{1}{8} =$

9. $\dfrac{5}{9} - \dfrac{4}{9} =$

10. $\dfrac{4}{6} - \dfrac{2}{6} =$

11. $\dfrac{3}{10} - \dfrac{1}{10} =$

12. $\dfrac{7}{9} - \dfrac{1}{9} =$

13. $\dfrac{3}{5} - \dfrac{2}{5} =$

14. $\dfrac{5}{7} - \dfrac{3}{7} =$

15. $\dfrac{2}{3} - \dfrac{1}{3} =$

16. $\dfrac{15}{16} - \dfrac{7}{16} =$

17. $\dfrac{4}{5} - \dfrac{2}{5} =$

18. $\dfrac{3}{6} - \dfrac{2}{6} =$

19. $\dfrac{2}{5} - \dfrac{1}{5} =$

20. $\dfrac{3}{4} - \dfrac{2}{4} =$

CD-104322 • © Carson-Dellosa

Subtracting Fractions with Like Denominators

Total Problems: **20**
Problems Correct: _____

Solve each problem. Write each answer in simplest form.

1. $\dfrac{2}{5} - \dfrac{1}{5} =$

2. $\dfrac{5}{7} - \dfrac{2}{7} =$

3. $\dfrac{3}{5} - \dfrac{1}{5} =$

4. $\dfrac{2}{8} - \dfrac{1}{8} =$

5. $\dfrac{2}{4} - \dfrac{1}{4} =$

6. $\dfrac{7}{8} - \dfrac{3}{8} =$

7. $\dfrac{2}{3} - \dfrac{1}{3} =$

8. $\dfrac{7}{9} - \dfrac{5}{9} =$

9. $\dfrac{4}{6} - \dfrac{1}{6} =$

10. $\dfrac{4}{7} - \dfrac{2}{7} =$

11. $\dfrac{7}{10} - \dfrac{3}{10} =$

12. $\dfrac{7}{8} - \dfrac{5}{8} =$

13. $\dfrac{3}{4} - \dfrac{2}{4} =$

14. $\dfrac{5}{9} - \dfrac{1}{9} =$

15. $\dfrac{4}{8} - \dfrac{1}{8} =$

16. $\dfrac{11}{14} - \dfrac{9}{14} =$

17. $\dfrac{5}{6} - \dfrac{1}{6} =$

18. $\dfrac{4}{5} - \dfrac{2}{5} =$

19. $\dfrac{1}{2} - \dfrac{1}{2} =$

20. $\dfrac{3}{5} - \dfrac{2}{5} =$

Subtracting Fractions with Unlike Denominators

Total Problems: **20**
Problems Correct: _____

Solve each problem. Write each answer in simplest form.

1. $\dfrac{3}{9}$
    $-\dfrac{1}{4}$

2. $\dfrac{3}{4}$
    $-\dfrac{1}{5}$

3. $\dfrac{4}{5}$
    $-\dfrac{5}{10}$

4. $\dfrac{5}{7}$
    $-\dfrac{2}{9}$

5. $\dfrac{2}{3}$
    $-\dfrac{4}{9}$

6. $\dfrac{3}{8}$
    $-\dfrac{2}{6}$

7. $\dfrac{2}{4}$
    $-\dfrac{1}{3}$

8. $\dfrac{1}{5}$
    $-\dfrac{1}{8}$

9. $\dfrac{7}{12}$
    $-\dfrac{1}{4}$

10. $\dfrac{3}{9}$
    $-\dfrac{1}{3}$

11. $\dfrac{7}{8}$
    $-\dfrac{1}{2}$

12. $\dfrac{8}{8}$
    $-\dfrac{4}{6}$

13. $\dfrac{2}{3}$
    $-\dfrac{1}{2}$

14. $\dfrac{1}{2}$
    $-\dfrac{1}{4}$

15. $\dfrac{1}{3}$
    $-\dfrac{1}{6}$

16. $\dfrac{8}{9}$
    $-\dfrac{3}{6}$

17. $\dfrac{5}{6}$
    $-\dfrac{1}{5}$

18. $\dfrac{7}{8}$
    $-\dfrac{3}{10}$

19. $\dfrac{9}{12}$
    $-\dfrac{2}{11}$

20. $\dfrac{6}{6}$
    $-\dfrac{3}{12}$

CD-104322 • © Carson-Dellosa

Name _____   Date _____

Subtracting Fractions with Unlike Denominators

Solve each problem. Write each answer in simplest form.

Total Problems: 20
Problems Correct: _____

1. $\frac{3}{4}$
    $-\frac{1}{6}$

2. $\frac{13}{15}$
    $-\frac{2}{3}$

3. $\frac{2}{3}$
    $-\frac{7}{12}$

4. $\frac{5}{6}$
    $-\frac{1}{3}$

5. $\frac{5}{6}$
    $-\frac{2}{5}$

6. $\frac{2}{3}$
    $-\frac{1}{6}$

7. $\frac{11}{14}$
    $-\frac{1}{2}$

8. $\frac{7}{12}$
    $-\frac{1}{4}$

9. $\frac{11}{12}$
    $-\frac{1}{6}$

10. $\frac{5}{6}$
    $-\frac{3}{7}$

11. $\frac{7}{8}$
    $-\frac{1}{9}$

12. $\frac{7}{8}$
    $-\frac{1}{2}$

13. $\frac{5}{12}$
    $-\frac{1}{3}$

14. $\frac{7}{8}$
    $-\frac{1}{6}$

15. $\frac{1}{3}$
    $-\frac{1}{6}$

16. $\frac{2}{3}$
    $-\frac{4}{9}$

17. $\frac{3}{4}$
    $-\frac{1}{3}$

18. $\frac{8}{9}$
    $-\frac{5}{6}$

19. $\frac{9}{12}$
    $-\frac{2}{11}$

20. $\frac{5}{6}$
    $-\frac{1}{8}$

Subtracting Fractions from Whole Numbers

Total Problems: **16**
Problems Correct: _____

Solve each problem. Write each answer in simplest form.

1. 2
$-\dfrac{7}{8}$

2. 3
$-\dfrac{3}{4}$

3. 5
$-\dfrac{6}{9}$

4. 12
$-\dfrac{5}{7}$

5. 4
$-\dfrac{2}{5}$

6. 8
$-\dfrac{9}{10}$

7. 4
$-\dfrac{2}{6}$

8. 9
$-\dfrac{1}{3}$

9. 5
$-\dfrac{2}{3}$

10. 7
$-\dfrac{4}{5}$

11. 5
$-\dfrac{2}{5}$

12. 4
$-\dfrac{7}{8}$

13. 6
$-\dfrac{1}{8}$

14. 4
$-\dfrac{3}{10}$

15. 10
$-\dfrac{1}{2}$

16. 3
$-\dfrac{6}{7}$

CD-104322 • © Carson-Dellosa

Name _____   Date _____

Subtracting Fractions from Whole Numbers

Total Problems: 16
Problems Correct: _____

Solve each problem. Write each answer in simplest form.

1. 15
    $-\ \dfrac{3}{8}$

2. 5
    $-\ \dfrac{3}{5}$

3. 1
    $-\ \dfrac{7}{8}$

4. 8
    $-\ \dfrac{3}{4}$

5. 10
    $-\ \dfrac{2}{5}$

6. 9
    $-\ \dfrac{3}{7}$

7. 6
    $-\ \dfrac{1}{5}$

8. 4
    $-\ \dfrac{1}{2}$

9. 1
    $-\ \dfrac{1}{3}$

10. 14
    $-\ \dfrac{2}{9}$

11. 7
    $-\ \dfrac{5}{6}$

12. 2
    $-\ \dfrac{1}{6}$

13. 2
    $-\ \dfrac{6}{11}$

14. 13
    $-\ \dfrac{2}{3}$

15. 5
    $-\ \dfrac{1}{4}$

16. 6
    $-\ \dfrac{3}{7}$

Subtracting Mixed Numbers with Like Denominators

Total Problems: **16**
Problems Correct: _____

Solve each problem. Write each answer in simplest form.

1. $8\frac{4}{5}$
$-1\frac{1}{5}$

2. $5\frac{3}{12}$
$-2\frac{17}{12}$

3. $5\frac{1}{3}$
$-4\frac{2}{3}$

4. $7\frac{3}{5}$
$-5\frac{1}{5}$

5. $5\frac{2}{3}$
$-4\frac{1}{3}$

6. $3\frac{3}{5}$
$-1\frac{4}{5}$

7. $5\frac{3}{8}$
$-3\frac{3}{8}$

8. $4\frac{11}{13}$
$-2\frac{12}{13}$

9. $3\frac{1}{2}$
$-1\frac{1}{2}$

10. $10\frac{9}{4}$
$-7\frac{1}{4}$

11. $9\frac{6}{7}$
$-2\frac{2}{7}$

12. $7\frac{1}{6}$
$-5\frac{3}{6}$

13. $4\frac{2}{6}$
$-3\frac{5}{6}$

14. $6\frac{7}{8}$
$-1\frac{1}{8}$

15. $2\frac{1}{8}$
$-1\frac{1}{8}$

16. $3\frac{7}{9}$
$-2\frac{1}{9}$

    CD-104322 • © Carson-Dellosa

Name _____ Date _____

Subtracting Mixed Numbers with Unlike Denominators

Total Problems: 16
Problems Correct: _____

Solve each problem. Write each answer in simplest form.

1. $12 \frac{7}{8}$
    $- 5 \frac{5}{16}$

2. $3 \frac{1}{4}$
    $- 2 \frac{5}{12}$

3. $10 \frac{2}{3}$
    $- 9 \frac{2}{9}$

4. $3 \frac{1}{8}$
    $- 1 \frac{7}{9}$

5. $10 \frac{2}{5}$
    $- 7 \frac{2}{3}$

6. $8 \frac{7}{10}$
    $- 7 \frac{9}{11}$

7. $8 \frac{5}{10}$
    $- 7 \frac{5}{12}$

8. $5 \frac{12}{16}$
    $- 5 \frac{11}{20}$

9. $6 \frac{1}{6}$
    $- 5 \frac{5}{12}$

10. $4 \frac{5}{6}$
    $- 2 \frac{1}{24}$

11. $8 \frac{3}{16}$
    $- 7 \frac{5}{32}$

12. $6 \frac{1}{9}$
    $- 2 \frac{1}{3}$

13. $2 \frac{2}{3}$
    $- 1 \frac{1}{5}$

14. $9 \frac{3}{5}$
    $- 4 \frac{9}{20}$

15. $4 \frac{11}{18}$
    $- 1 \frac{13}{16}$

16. $8 \frac{7}{10}$
    $- 6 \frac{3}{40}$

Multiplying Fractions

Solve each problem. Write each answer in simplest form.

1. $\dfrac{1}{4} \times \dfrac{2}{5} =$

2. $\dfrac{2}{8} \times \dfrac{3}{6} =$

3. $\dfrac{1}{6} \times \dfrac{4}{5} =$

4. $\dfrac{1}{3} \times \dfrac{5}{6} =$

5. $\dfrac{4}{6} \times \dfrac{5}{7} =$

6. $\dfrac{3}{5} \times \dfrac{1}{8} =$

7. $\dfrac{5}{7} \times \dfrac{2}{4} =$

8. $\dfrac{3}{4} \times \dfrac{4}{7} =$

9. $\dfrac{3}{4} \times \dfrac{5}{5} =$

10. $\dfrac{1}{6} \times \dfrac{4}{5} =$

11. $\dfrac{5}{6} \times \dfrac{3}{4} =$

12. $\dfrac{3}{5} \times \dfrac{3}{7} =$

13. $\dfrac{2}{5} \times \dfrac{4}{9} =$

14. $\dfrac{2}{8} \times \dfrac{3}{3} =$

15. $\dfrac{1}{7} \times \dfrac{3}{4} =$

CD-104322 • © Carson-Dellosa

Multiplying Fractions

Total Problems: 15
Problems Correct: _____

Solve each problem. Write each answer in simplest form.

1. $\dfrac{5}{8} \times \dfrac{3}{4} =$

2. $\dfrac{3}{4} \times \dfrac{2}{7} =$

3. $\dfrac{5}{7} \times \dfrac{3}{7} =$

4. $\dfrac{1}{2} \times \dfrac{3}{5} =$

5. $\dfrac{3}{6} \times \dfrac{7}{8} =$

6. $\dfrac{2}{9} \times \dfrac{4}{6} =$

7. $\dfrac{1}{2} \times \dfrac{5}{9} =$

8. $\dfrac{3}{8} \times \dfrac{1}{4} =$

9. $\dfrac{1}{4} \times \dfrac{3}{7} =$

10. $\dfrac{4}{5} \times \dfrac{5}{6} =$

11. $\dfrac{1}{2} \times \dfrac{3}{7} =$

12. $\dfrac{2}{3} \times \dfrac{3}{5} =$

13. $\dfrac{2}{6} \times \dfrac{2}{5} =$

14. $\dfrac{8}{9} \times \dfrac{1}{6} =$

15. $\dfrac{3}{6} \times \dfrac{8}{9} =$

Multiplying Fractions

Solve each problem. Write each answer in simplest form.

1. $\dfrac{3}{4} \times \dfrac{2}{5} =$

2. $\dfrac{7}{8} \times \dfrac{1}{6} =$

3. $\dfrac{4}{5} \times \dfrac{2}{3} =$

4. $\dfrac{1}{3} \times \dfrac{1}{5} =$

5. $\dfrac{2}{7} \times \dfrac{2}{9} =$

6. $\dfrac{1}{4} \times \dfrac{3}{5} =$

7. $\dfrac{4}{7} \times \dfrac{3}{8} =$

8. $\dfrac{2}{3} \times \dfrac{2}{5} =$

9. $\dfrac{1}{3} \times \dfrac{4}{5} =$

10. $\dfrac{3}{5} \times \dfrac{1}{3} =$

11. $\dfrac{1}{8} \times \dfrac{2}{5} =$

12. $\dfrac{1}{6} \times \dfrac{2}{3} =$

13. $\dfrac{1}{2} \times \dfrac{3}{4} =$

14. $\dfrac{1}{8} \times \dfrac{1}{3} =$

15. $\dfrac{2}{8} \times \dfrac{3}{4} =$

CD-104322 • © Carson-Dellosa

Multiplying Fractions

| Total Problems: | 15 |
| Problems Correct: | _____ |

Solve each problem. Write each answer in simplest form.

1. $\dfrac{1}{3} \times \dfrac{1}{7} =$

2. $\dfrac{3}{5} \times \dfrac{2}{9} =$

3. $\dfrac{1}{6} \times \dfrac{4}{5} =$

4. $\dfrac{2}{7} \times \dfrac{5}{8} =$

5. $\dfrac{2}{5} \times \dfrac{4}{9} =$

6. $\dfrac{1}{4} \times \dfrac{1}{6} =$

7. $\dfrac{2}{3} \times \dfrac{3}{8} =$

8. $\dfrac{3}{4} \times \dfrac{4}{7} =$

9. $\dfrac{2}{5} \times \dfrac{5}{6} =$

10. $\dfrac{4}{5} \times \dfrac{2}{3} =$

11. $\dfrac{1}{5} \times \dfrac{5}{6} =$

12. $\dfrac{1}{2} \times \dfrac{3}{7} =$

13. $\dfrac{2}{5} \times \dfrac{5}{9} =$

14. $\dfrac{2}{8} \times \dfrac{3}{3} =$

15. $\dfrac{5}{6} \times \dfrac{2}{7} =$

Multiplying Fractions and Whole Numbers

Solve each problem. Write each answer in simplest form.

Total Problems: **15**
Problems Correct: _____

1. $4 \times \dfrac{1}{2} =$

2. $2 \times \dfrac{2}{5} =$

3. $4 \times \dfrac{2}{7} =$

4. $3 \times \dfrac{5}{6} =$

5. $8 \times \dfrac{1}{8} =$

6. $\dfrac{2}{5} \times 3 =$

7. $\dfrac{1}{8} \times 5 =$

8. $\dfrac{5}{7} \times 5 =$

9. $\dfrac{2}{3} \times 2 =$

10. $\dfrac{3}{9} \times 4 =$

11. $\dfrac{1}{3} \times 7 =$

12. $4 \times \dfrac{3}{4} =$

13. $\dfrac{6}{8} \times 2 =$

14. $5 \times \dfrac{4}{5} =$

15. $8 \times \dfrac{2}{5} =$

CD-104322 • © Carson-Dellosa

Multiplying Fractions and Whole Numbers

Solve each problem. Write each answer in simplest form.

Total Problems: **15**
Problems Correct: _____

1. $5 \times \frac{2}{5} =$

2. $8 \times \frac{1}{7} =$

3. $6 \times \frac{3}{8} =$

4. $4 \times \frac{8}{9} =$

5. $2 \times \frac{3}{7} =$

6. $\frac{2}{3} \times 4 =$

7. $\frac{1}{9} \times 6 =$

8. $\frac{5}{6} \times 4 =$

9. $\frac{4}{6} \times 3 =$

10. $\frac{4}{5} \times 6 =$

11. $\frac{3}{4} \times 5 =$

12. $2 \times \frac{4}{5} =$

13. $\frac{2}{7} \times 6 =$

14. $7 \times \frac{3}{5} =$

15. $9 \times \frac{3}{4} =$

Multiplying Fractions and Whole Numbers

Solve each problem. Write each answer in simplest form.

1. $10 \times \dfrac{2}{3} =$

2. $4 \times \dfrac{4}{7} =$

3. $7 \times \dfrac{10}{11} =$

4. $36 \times \dfrac{2}{288} =$

5. $6 \times \dfrac{4}{8} =$

6. $9 \times \dfrac{5}{6} =$

7. $3 \times \dfrac{1}{3} =$

8. $30 \times \dfrac{3}{90} =$

9. $12 \times \dfrac{1}{36} =$

10. $5 \times \dfrac{2}{5} =$

11. $12 \times \dfrac{7}{8} =$

12. $5 \times \dfrac{3}{4} =$

13. $22 \times \dfrac{1}{44} =$

14. $4 \times \dfrac{1}{8} =$

15. $11 \times \dfrac{3}{8} =$

CD-104322 • © Carson-Dellosa

Multiplying Mixed Numbers and Whole Numbers

Total Problems: **12**
Problems Correct: _____

Solve each problem. Write each answer in simplest form.

1. $2 \times 2\frac{1}{3} =$

2. $3 \times 5\frac{1}{5} =$

3. $9 \times 3\frac{2}{3} =$

4. $8 \times 9\frac{1}{10} =$

5. $4 \times 5\frac{1}{8} =$

6. $6 \times 3\frac{1}{6} =$

7. $5 \times 6\frac{5}{8} =$

8. $3 \times 9\frac{1}{3} =$

9. $7 \times 1\frac{3}{4} =$

10. $7 \times 2\frac{3}{5} =$

11. $4 \times 2\frac{1}{2} =$

12. $7 \times 2\frac{1}{7} =$

Multiplying Mixed Numbers and Whole Numbers

Solve each problem. Write each answer in simplest form.

Total Problems: **12**
Problems Correct: _____

1. $4 \times 3\frac{3}{5} =$

2. $6 \times 9\frac{4}{5} =$

3. $2 \times 8\frac{3}{4} =$

4. $9 \times 1\frac{1}{18} =$

5. $10 \times 5\frac{1}{2} =$

6. $8 \times 2\frac{3}{8} =$

7. $5 \times 4\frac{2}{5} =$

8. $2 \times 7\frac{5}{8} =$

9. $2 \times 5\frac{1}{8} =$

10. $3 \times 1\frac{15}{16} =$

11. $4 \times 8\frac{6}{7} =$

12. $2 \times 2\frac{1}{4} =$

   CD-104322 • © Carson-Dellosa

Multiplying Mixed Numbers

Total Problems: **12**
Problems Correct: _____

Solve each problem. Write each answer in simplest form.

1. $3\frac{1}{2} \times 2\frac{1}{2} =$

2. $8\frac{5}{6} \times 3\frac{6}{7} =$

3. $4\frac{2}{5} \times 6\frac{2}{3} =$

4. $4\frac{2}{9} \times 5\frac{10}{11} =$

5. $2\frac{2}{3} \times 4\frac{2}{5} =$

6. $5\frac{3}{4} \times 6\frac{1}{4} =$

7. $2\frac{8}{9} \times 7\frac{7}{8} =$

8. $7\frac{1}{4} \times 3\frac{3}{7} =$

9. $6\frac{7}{8} \times 3\frac{1}{3} =$

10. $7\frac{9}{10} \times 8\frac{7}{8} =$

11. $4\frac{1}{4} \times 3\frac{5}{6} =$

12. $8\frac{3}{5} \times 1\frac{1}{2} =$

Multiplying Mixed Numbers

Total Problems: **12**
Problems Correct: _____

Solve each problem. Write each answer in simplest form.

1. $8\frac{1}{4} \times 6\frac{2}{3} =$

2. $7\frac{2}{5} \times 9\frac{1}{8} =$

3. $2\frac{5}{6} \times 12\frac{4}{5} =$

4. $4\frac{2}{7} \times 6\frac{1}{10} =$

5. $2\frac{9}{10} \times 5\frac{7}{8} =$

6. $5\frac{1}{3} \times 4\frac{1}{2} =$

7. $3\frac{1}{3} \times 3\frac{1}{3} =$

8. $3\frac{3}{4} \times 2\frac{1}{3} =$

9. $5\frac{1}{5} \times 4\frac{1}{3} =$

10. $9\frac{9}{10} \times 4\frac{7}{8} =$

11. $1\frac{10}{13} \times 2\frac{9}{13} =$

12. $8\frac{3}{5} \times 4\frac{5}{6} =$

CD-104322 • © Carson-Dellosa

Name _____   Date _____

Finding the Reciprocal

Total Problems: **16**
Problems Correct: _____

Find the reciprocal of each fraction or whole number.

1. $\frac{3}{5}$ _____

2. $\frac{2}{3}$ _____

3. 9 _____

4. $\frac{5}{3}$ _____

5. $\frac{7}{3}$ _____

6. $\frac{6}{3}$ _____

7. $\frac{1}{12}$ _____

8. $\frac{9}{10}$ _____

9. $\frac{2}{17}$ _____

10. $\frac{9}{1}$ _____

11. 6 _____

12. $\frac{4}{2}$ _____

Change each mixed number to an improper fraction. Then, find its reciprocal.

	Fraction	**Reciprocal**
13. $2\frac{3}{5}$ =	_____	_____
14. $1\frac{3}{4}$ =	_____	_____
15. $3\frac{7}{8}$ =	_____	_____
16. $6\frac{2}{5}$ =	_____	_____

Dividing Fractions

Total Problems: **15**
Problems Correct: _____

Solve each problem. Write each answer in simplest form.

1. $\dfrac{3}{5} \div \dfrac{5}{6} =$

2. $\dfrac{5}{8} \div \dfrac{3}{5} =$

3. $\dfrac{7}{10} \div \dfrac{3}{5} =$

4. $\dfrac{4}{7} \div \dfrac{3}{7} =$

5. $\dfrac{3}{5} \div \dfrac{7}{8} =$

6. $\dfrac{3}{16} \div \dfrac{3}{8} =$

7. $\dfrac{4}{9} \div \dfrac{3}{4} =$

8. $\dfrac{7}{8} \div \dfrac{2}{3} =$

9. $\dfrac{1}{6} \div \dfrac{4}{5} =$

10. $\dfrac{3}{4} \div \dfrac{3}{5} =$

11. $\dfrac{7}{9} \div \dfrac{2}{3} =$

12. $\dfrac{7}{8} \div \dfrac{5}{11} =$

13. $\dfrac{2}{5} \div \dfrac{3}{8} =$

14. $\dfrac{2}{3} \div \dfrac{4}{5} =$

15. $\dfrac{5}{9} \div \dfrac{2}{8} =$

CD-104322 • © Carson-Dellosa

Dividing Fractions and Whole Numbers

Solve each problem. Write each answer in simplest form.

Total Problems: 15
Problems Correct: _____

1. $8 \div \dfrac{6}{7} =$

2. $3 \div \dfrac{1}{2} =$

3. $12 \div \dfrac{3}{4} =$

4. $14 \div \dfrac{7}{8} =$

5. $5 \div \dfrac{1}{3} =$

6. $\dfrac{5}{6} \div 10 =$

7. $\dfrac{2}{3} \div 6 =$

8. $\dfrac{3}{4} \div 4 =$

9. $\dfrac{1}{2} \div 6 =$

10. $\dfrac{1}{4} \div 2 =$

11. $\dfrac{2}{5} \div 3 =$

12. $10 \div \dfrac{6}{7} =$

13. $\dfrac{4}{7} \div 5 =$

14. $6 \div \dfrac{1}{5} =$

15. $12 \div \dfrac{3}{9} =$

Dividing Fractions and Mixed Numbers

Total Problems: **12**
Problems Correct: _____

Solve each problem. Write each answer in simplest form.

1. $1\frac{1}{6} \div \frac{1}{4} =$

2. $3\frac{1}{4} \div \frac{3}{8} =$

3. $5\frac{2}{3} \div \frac{9}{10} =$

4. $1\frac{4}{5} \div \frac{2}{7} =$

5. $2\frac{3}{4} \div \frac{1}{8} =$

6. $2\frac{1}{2} \div \frac{1}{2} =$

7. $2\frac{1}{4} \div \frac{3}{8} =$

8. $4\frac{1}{2} \div \frac{1}{2} =$

9. $6\frac{1}{8} \div \frac{4}{7} =$

10. $2\frac{3}{4} \div \frac{1}{2} =$

11. $1\frac{1}{4} \div \frac{2}{3} =$

12. $1\frac{2}{5} \div \frac{1}{3} =$

Dividing Fractions and Mixed Numbers

Solve each problem. Write each answer in simplest form.

1. $1\dfrac{1}{6} \div \dfrac{1}{4} =$

2. $2\dfrac{2}{5} \div \dfrac{2}{3} =$

3. $6\dfrac{3}{8} \div \dfrac{7}{10} =$

4. $1\dfrac{1}{3} \div \dfrac{7}{8} =$

5. $3\dfrac{1}{2} \div \dfrac{1}{4} =$

6. $5\dfrac{1}{3} \div \dfrac{3}{8} =$

7. $3\dfrac{1}{3} \div \dfrac{3}{4} =$

8. $2\dfrac{1}{3} \div 5 =$

9. $1\dfrac{1}{3} \div \dfrac{8}{3} =$

10. $3\dfrac{3}{5} \div 10 =$

11. $1\dfrac{1}{5} \div \dfrac{2}{5} =$

12. $5\dfrac{6}{7} \div \dfrac{3}{4} =$

Dividing Mixed Numbers

Total Problems: 12
Problems Correct: _____

Solve each problem. Write each answer in simplest form.

1. $2\frac{1}{3} \div 4\frac{1}{5} =$

2. $5\frac{1}{2} \div 1\frac{1}{8} =$

3. $3\frac{1}{3} \div 1\frac{1}{9} =$

4. $2\frac{2}{3} \div 2\frac{2}{5} =$

5. $5\frac{1}{4} \div 2\frac{1}{3} =$

6. $7\frac{3}{8} \div 1\frac{5}{8} =$

7. $5\frac{2}{3} \div 1\frac{6}{7} =$

8. $2\frac{2}{5} \div 3\frac{7}{10} =$

9. $6\frac{1}{3} \div 3\frac{5}{6} =$

10. $6\frac{3}{8} \div 2\frac{5}{6} =$

11. $7\frac{1}{9} \div 5\frac{1}{3} =$

12. $7\frac{2}{5} \div 5\frac{2}{3} =$

CD-104322 • © Carson-Dellosa

Dividing Mixed Numbers

Total Problems: **12**
Problems Correct: _____

Solve each problem. Write each answer in simplest form.

1. $8\frac{3}{4} \div 5\frac{2}{5} =$

2. $9\frac{3}{5} \div 8\frac{2}{3} =$

3. $3\frac{1}{3} \div 5\frac{3}{5} =$

4. $1\frac{3}{7} \div 2\frac{2}{3} =$

5. $1\frac{3}{5} \div 2\frac{1}{2} =$

6. $2\frac{1}{5} \div 1\frac{3}{4} =$

7. $2\frac{1}{2} \div 3\frac{8}{9} =$

8. $4\frac{2}{3} \div 5\frac{9}{10} =$

9. $3\frac{3}{5} \div 3\frac{3}{4} =$

10. $5\frac{2}{5} \div 6\frac{5}{8} =$

11. $6\frac{3}{4} \div 2\frac{5}{8} =$

12. $4\frac{3}{8} \div 3\frac{3}{5} =$

Multiplying and Dividing Fractions Review

Total Problems: **12**
Problems Correct: _____

Solve each problem. Write each answer in simplest form.

1. $1\frac{1}{3} \div 2\frac{1}{2} =$

2. $6\frac{7}{8} \div 1\frac{1}{3} =$

3. $3\frac{1}{5} \times 2\frac{1}{10} =$

4. $1\frac{4}{5} \times 3\frac{5}{5} =$

5. $1\frac{4}{5} \div 1\frac{1}{5} =$

6. $2\frac{1}{2} \div 1\frac{1}{2} =$

7. $2\frac{1}{3} \times 3\frac{1}{3} =$

8. $4\frac{2}{6} \times 3\frac{7}{18} =$

9. $2\frac{3}{5} \times 1\frac{1}{2} =$

10. $4\frac{1}{2} \div 1\frac{1}{5} =$

11. $3\frac{3}{4} \times 2\frac{2}{6} =$

12. $3\frac{3}{8} \div 3\frac{3}{8} =$

CD-104322 • © Carson-Dellosa

Name _____   Date _____

Multiplying and Dividing Fractions Review

Total Problems: **12**
Problems Correct: _____

Solve each problem. Write each answer in simplest form.

1. $3\frac{1}{3} \div 1\frac{1}{2} =$

2. $5\frac{1}{2} \div 1\frac{1}{4} =$

3. $2\frac{1}{6} \times 1\frac{1}{12} =$

4. $2\frac{3}{6} \times 4\frac{5}{10} =$

5. $2\frac{3}{5} \div 2\frac{1}{5} =$

6. $2\frac{1}{4} \times 1\frac{1}{4} =$

7. $3\frac{2}{4} \div 1\frac{1}{5} =$

8. $2\frac{2}{8} \times 4\frac{5}{16} =$

9. $3\frac{1}{2} \times 3\frac{1}{2} =$

10. $4\frac{1}{6} \div 1\frac{1}{6} =$

11. $2\frac{3}{5} \div 1\frac{2}{5} =$

12. $3\frac{3}{5} \times 3\frac{3}{5} =$

Understanding Decimals

Total Problems: **11**
Problems Correct: _____

Complete the chart. Fill in the whole number, tenths, hundredths, and thousandths columns with the correct number. Use zeros as placeholders where necessary.

	Number	Whole Number	Tenths	Hundredths	Thousandths
1.	3.751				
2.	4.891				
3.	1.608				
4.	10.540				
5.	9.618				
6.	2.198				
7.	0.208				
8.	0.005				
9.	1.7				
10.	2.398				
11.	6.0				

CD-104322 • © Carson-Dellosa

Understanding Decimals

Write a decimal for each of the following descriptions.

1. One tenth _____

2. Twenty-seven hundredths _____

3. Three thousandths _____

4. Seven tenths _____

5. Forty-five hundredths _____

6. Fifty-one thousandths _____

Write each decimal in words.

7. 0.047 _____

8. 0.99 _____

9. 0.8 _____

10. 0.809 _____

11. 0.06 _____

Order the numbers in each series from smallest to largest.

12. 1.871, 0.1871, 10.871 _____

13. 0.045, 0.45, 0.04 _____

14. 0.0065, 0.06, 0.006 _____

15. 0.91, 0.44, 0.23 _____

16. 6.07, 6.17, 6.37 _____

Writing Decimals as Fractions

Total Problems: **16**
Problems Correct: _____

Write each decimal as a fraction. Write the answer in simplest form.

1. $0.25 =$

2. $0.15 =$

3. $0.035 =$

4. $0.17 =$

5. $0.75 =$

6. $0.30 =$

7. $0.125 =$

8. $0.50 =$

9. $0.033 =$

10. $0.075 =$

11. $0.60 =$

12. $0.018 =$

13. $0.6 =$

14. $0.025 =$

15. $0.185 =$

16. $0.611 =$

CD-104322 • © Carson-Dellosa

Writing Decimals as Fractions

Total Problems: 16
Problems Correct: _____

Write each decimal as a fraction. Write the answer in simplest form.

1. $0.625 =$ **2.** $0.008 =$ **3.** $0.60 =$ **4.** $0.23 =$

5. $0.020 =$ **6.** $0.054 =$ **7.** $0.075 =$ **8.** $0.001 =$

9. $0.100 =$ **10.** $0.012 =$ **11.** $0.033 =$ **12.** $0.12 =$

13. $0.03 =$ **14.** $0.219 =$ **15.** $0.575 =$ **16.** $0.35 =$

Writing Decimals as Fractions

Total Problems: **16**
Problems Correct: _____

Write each decimal as a fraction. Write the answer in simplest form.

1. $0.5 =$

2. $0.05 =$

3. $0.075 =$

4. $0.12 =$

5. $0.333 =$

6. $0.25 =$

7. $0.15 =$

8. $0.54 =$

9. $0.1 =$

10. $0.08 =$

11. $0.125 =$

12. $0.2 =$

13. $0.8 =$

14. $0.143 =$

15. $0.625 =$

16. $0.025 =$

CD-104322 • © Carson-Dellosa

Writing Decimals as Fractions

Write each decimal as a fraction or mixed number. Write the
answer in simplest form.

Total Problems: **16**
Problems Correct: _____

1. 0.009 =

2. 0.41 =

3. 3.5 =

4. 4.014 =

5. 0.019 =

6. 0.15 =

7. 4.03 =

8. 0.5 =

9. 0.933 =

10. 0.183 =

11. 2.62 =

12. 0.09 =

13. 0.3 =

14. 0.025 =

15. 3.25 =

16. 6.17 =

Writing Fractions as Decimals

Total Problems: **12**
Problems Correct: _____

Write each fraction or mixed number as a decimal.

1. $\dfrac{6}{10} =$

2. $\dfrac{3}{10} =$

3. $3\dfrac{8}{10} =$

4. $4\dfrac{15}{1,000} =$

5. $\dfrac{7}{100} =$

6. $\dfrac{4}{100} =$

7. $2\dfrac{9}{10} =$

8. $\dfrac{8}{1,000} =$

9. $\dfrac{27}{100} =$

10. $\dfrac{50}{100} =$

11. $\dfrac{142}{1,000} =$

12. $\dfrac{7}{100} =$

CD-104322 • © Carson-Dellosa

Name _____ Date _____

Writing Fractions as Decimals

Total Problems: **16**
Problems Correct: _____

Write each fraction or mixed number as a decimal. Round to the nearest thousandth when necessary.

1. $5\frac{7}{8} =$

2. $\frac{47}{50}$ —

3. $\frac{1}{2} =$

4. $\frac{9}{200}$ —

5. $3\frac{4}{5} =$

6. $\frac{3}{8} =$

7. $\frac{1}{5} =$

8. $\frac{7}{25} =$

9. $4\frac{3}{5} =$

10. $\frac{3}{4} =$

11. $\frac{1}{4} =$

12. $\frac{7}{20} =$

13. $2\frac{1}{5} =$

14. $\frac{1}{8} =$

15. $\frac{1}{3} =$

16. $\frac{4}{5} =$

Name _____   Date _____

Adding Decimals

Total Problems: **20**
Problems Correct: _____

Solve each problem.

1. 2.4
  + 1.7

2. 18.6
  + 9.5

3. 0.01
  + 0.72

4. 3.2
  1.4
  + 7.8

5. 2.016
  3.094
  + 8.627

6. 8.1
  + 9.2

7. 14.3
  + 1.9

8. 1.04
  + 2.07

9. 86.7
  5.2
  + 8.4

10. 42.65
  67.23
  + 12.12

11. 10.3
  + 7.4

12. 24.7
  + 32.6

13. 16.52
  + 13.63

14. 9.1
  12.5
  + 19.4

15. 492.6
  382.3
  + 225.7

16. 1.5
  + 1.5

17. 20.5
  + 32.3

18. 14.87
  + 56.09

19. 40.08
  60.27
  + 50.33

20. 4.008
  1.318
  + 0.056

CD-104322 • © Carson-Dellosa

Name _____ Date _____

Adding Decimals

Total Problems: **16**
Problems Correct: _____

Solve each problem.

1. 2.34
    0.02
    + 1.65

2. 543.7
      3.42
    +   0.06

3. 72.56
    12.38
    + 0.07

4. 22.87
    45.7
    + 1.26

5. 987.5
      4.1
    + 30.2

6.   2.14
      0.007
    + 72.4

7.   1.70
    23.75
    + 0.605

8. 86.15
      0.07
    + 5.72

9.   5.1
      7.53
    + 87.4

10. 0.2
     1.2
    + 0.12

11.   1.45
     20.03
    + 0.17

12.   4.5
       5.4
    + 12.67

13. 42.7
     0.03
    + 1.7

14. 87.5
       1.2
    + 591.35

15. 0.725
     1.33
    + 12

16. 42
     0.543
    + 7.8

Subtracting Decimals

Total Problems: **20**
Problems Correct: _____

Solve each problem.

1. 0.8
   − 0.4

2. 0.47
   − 0.21

3. 0.753
   − 0.211

4. 4.6
   − 2.1

5. 42.53
   − 0.25

6. 0.9
   − 0.5

7. 0.53
   − 0.27

8. 0.867
   − 0.501

9. 5.6
   − 0.2

10. 87.54
    − 6.25

11. 0.3
    − 0.1

12. 0.37
    − 0.15

13. 0.467
    − 0.338

14. 37.6
    − 0.7

15. 95.43
    − 16.07

16. 0.5
    − 0.2

17. 0.42
    − 0.12

18. 0.575
    − 0.104

19. 25.06
    − 3.72

20. 53.27
    − 5.42

CD-104322 • © Carson-Dellosa

Name _____   Date _____

Subtracting Decimals

Total Problems: **16**
Problems Correct: _____

Solve each problem.

1. 19.867
      – 1.07

2. 4.52
      – 0.4

3. 6.254
      – 3.01

4. 23.154
      – 3.08

5. 0.7
      – 0.506

6. 20.342
      – 0.37

7. 756.83
      – 22.5

8. 38.7
      – 5.21

9. 1.428
      – 1.2

10. 71.34
       – 2.672

11. 31.1
       – 3.052

12. 0.65
       – 0.224

13. 2.3
       – 1.437

14. 32.456
       – 1.2

15. 81.384
       – 2.777

16. 24.75
       – 6.243

Multiplying Decimals

Total Problems: 20
Problems Correct: _____

Solve each problem. Round to the nearest thousandth when necessary.

1. 0.2
  $\times\ 4$

2. 0.08
  $\times\ \ 6$

3. 5.7
  $\times\ 0.9$

4. 0.14
  $\times\ 0.27$

5. 0.67
  $\times\ 5.4$

6. 0.8
  $\times\ 3$

7. 0.04
  $\times\ \ 5$

8. 4.3
  $\times\ 2$

9. 7.2
  $\times\ 5.3$

10. 7.1
  $\times\ 5.5$

11. 0.5
  $\times\ 0.4$

12. 6
  $\times\ 0.12$

13. 1.07
  $\times\ 0.55$

14. 0.09
  $\times\ 0.06$

15. 0.07
  $\times\ 0.15$

16. 0.23
  $\times\ 0.7$

17. 0.5
  $\times\ 0.25$

18. 2.15
  $\times\ 0.8$

19. 1.3
  $\times\ 3.1$

20. 32
  $\times\ 6.4$

CD-104322 • © Carson-Dellosa

Name _____   Date _____

Multiplying Decimals

Total Problems: **16**
Problems Correct: _____

Solve each problem. Round to the nearest thousandth
when necessary.

1. 0.187
  × 1.5

2. 0.156
  × 100

3. 0.0708
  × 0.42

4. 87.859
  × 63.4

5. 1.709
  × 536.7

6. 6.42
  × 3.7

7. 0.487
  × 13.5

8. 0.1065
  × 53.7

9. 4.06
  × 0.7

10. 43.6
  × 64.7

11. 80.42
  × 7.86

12. 0.622
  × 5.97

13. 84.4
  × 0.007

14. 5.11
  × 0.78

15. 4.35
  × 0.682

16. 3.187
  × 0.78

Dividing Decimals

Total Problems: **20**
Problems Correct: _____

Solve each problem.

1. $9\overline{)2.7}$

2. $7\overline{)2.1}$

3. $4\overline{)0.16}$

4. $0.8\overline{)56}$

5. $6\overline{)3.6}$

6. $8\overline{)0.64}$

7. $9\overline{)0.27}$

8. $0.07\overline{)2.1}$

9. $3\overline{)2.7}$

10. $6\overline{)0.30}$

11. $0.04\overline{)28}$

12. $0.9\overline{)5.4}$

13. $3\overline{)0.18}$

14. $2\overline{)0.12}$

15. $0.9\overline{)72}$

16. $0.7\overline{)0.35}$

17. $4\overline{)2.4}$

18. $5\overline{)2.5}$

19. $0.04\overline{)36}$

20. $0.9\overline{)6.3}$

CD-104322 • © Carson-Dellosa

Dividing Decimals

Total Problems: **16**
Problems Correct: _____

Solve each problem.

1. $4\overline{)9.6}$

2. $0.5\overline{)12.5}$

3. $16\overline{)59.2}$

4. $1.8\overline{)57.6}$

5. $0.15\overline{)75}$

6. $1.2\overline{)1.44}$

7. $1.3\overline{)1.30}$

8. $0.09\overline{)0.783}$

9. $0.2\overline{)1}$

10. $3\overline{)0.363}$

11. $0.27\overline{)648}$

12. $5.2\overline{)13.52}$

13. $0.06\overline{)1.20}$

14. $5.4\overline{)64.8}$

15. $0.5\overline{)10.50}$

16. $6.7\overline{)33.5}$

Finding Percents

Total Problems: 25
Problems Correct: _____

Write each fraction as a percent.

1. $\frac{1}{2} =$

2. $\frac{9}{20} =$

3. $\frac{3}{4} =$

4. $\frac{6}{25} =$

5. $\frac{1}{5} =$

6. $\frac{2}{5} =$

7. $\frac{9}{10} =$

8. $\frac{1}{10} =$

9. $\frac{1}{4} =$

10. $\frac{4}{25} =$

Write each percent as a fraction. Write each answer in simplest form.

11. $16\% =$

12. $35\% =$

13. $77\% =$

14. $90\% =$

15. $25\% =$

16. $33\% =$

17. $28\% =$

18. $10\% =$

19. $5\% =$

20. $14\% =$

21. $75\% =$

22. $9\% =$

23. $40\% =$

24. $55\% =$

25. $99\% =$

CD-104322 • © Carson-Dellosa

Finding Percents

Total Problems: **20**
Problems Correct: _____

Write each decimal as a percent.

1. 0.9 =

2. 0.007 =

3. 0.52 =

4. 0.462 =

5. 0.062 =

6. 0.1283 =

7. 0.321 =

8. 0.505 =

9. 0.65 =

10. 0.3 =

Write each percent as a decimal.

11. 10% =

12. 0.45% =

13. 16.2% =

14. 98% =

15. 3.5% =

16. 2.75% =

17. 8% =

18. 10.3% =

19. 12.5% =

20. 1.75% =

Finding Percents

Total Problems: **15**
Problems Correct: _____

Find the given percent of each number.

1. 10% of 50 =

2. 50% of 48 =

3. 40% of 80 =

4. 60% of 90 =

5. 16% of 64 =

6. 70% of 25 =

7. 25% of 50 =

8. 20% of 100 =

9. 32% of 94 =

10. 15% of 45 =

11. 85% of 20 =

12. 5% of 57 =

13. 97% of 63 =

14. 13% of 87 =

15. 12% of 32 =

CD-104322 • © Carson-Dellosa

Fractions, Decimals, and Percents Review

Total Problems: **20**
Problems Correct: _____

Write each fraction as a decimal.

1. $\dfrac{13}{20} =$ **2.** $\dfrac{9}{5} =$ **3.** $\dfrac{4}{25} =$ **4.** $\dfrac{43}{50} =$

Write each percent as a fraction.

5. $28\% =$ **6.** $64\% =$ **7.** $15\% =$ **8.** $65\% =$

Write each decimal as a percent.

9. $0.005 =$ **10.** $0.128 =$ **11.** $0.27 =$ **12.** $0.6 =$

Change each percent to a decimal.

13. $13.6\% =$ **14.** $84\% =$ **15.** $0.37\% =$ **16.** $5\% =$

Find the given percent of each number.

17. 6% of $25 =$ **18.** 80% of $50 =$

19. 9% of $100 =$ **20.** 15% of $30 =$

Fractions, Decimals, and Percents Review

Complete the chart. Round to the nearest thousandth when necessary.

	Fraction	Decimal	Percentage
1.			17%
2.		0.5	
3.	$\frac{13}{17}$		
4.		0.95	
5.			75%
6.		0.125	
7.	$\frac{1}{6}$		
8.		0.005	
9.			30%
10.		0.45	

Name _____   Date _____

Finding the Perimeter of a Polygon

┌─────────────────────────┐
Total Problems: **6**
Problems Correct: _____
└─────────────────────────┘

Find the perimeter of each figure.

1. Perimeter = _____

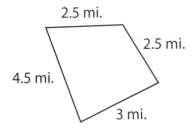

2. Perimeter = _____

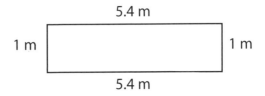

3. Perimeter = _____

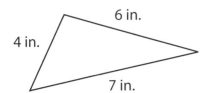

4. Perimeter = _____

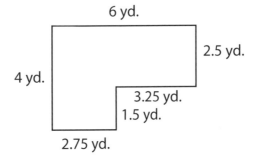

5. Perimeter = _____

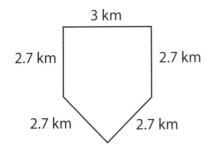

6. Perimeter = _____

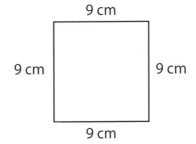

Name _____   Date _____

Finding the Area of a Rectangle

Total Problems: **6**
Problems Correct: _____

Find the area of each rectangle. Use the formula:
A = length × width.

1. Area = _____

7 mi.

7 mi.

2. Area = _____

36 cm

40 cm

3. Area = _____

8 yd.

4.7 yd.

4. Area = _____

5 in.

5 in.

5. Area = _____

9 m

3.8 m

6. Area = _____

8 ft.

5.3 ft.

CD-104322 • © Carson-Dellosa

Name _____   Date _____

Finding the Area of a Triangle

Total Problems: 6
Problems Correct: _____

Find the area of each triangle. Use the formula:
$A = \frac{1}{2} \times$ (**base × height**).

1. Area = _____

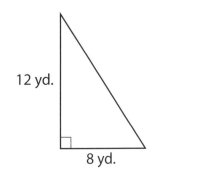

12 yd.

8 yd.

2. Area = _____

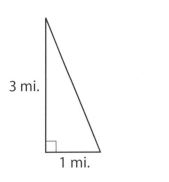

3 mi.

1 mi.

3. Area = _____

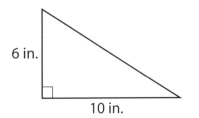

6 in.

10 in.

4. Area = _____

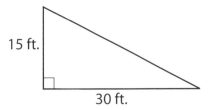

15 ft.

30 ft.

5. Area = _____

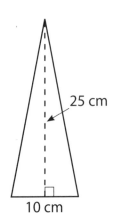

25 cm

10 cm

6. Area = _____

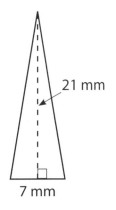

21 mm

7 mm

Name _____   Date _____

Finding the Volume of a Rectangular Prism

Total Problems: **6**
Problems Correct: _____

Find the volume of each rectangular prism. Use the formula:
Volume = length × width × height.

1. Volume = _____

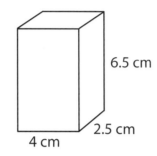

2. Volume = _____

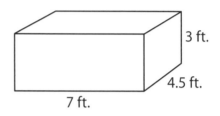

3. Volume = _____

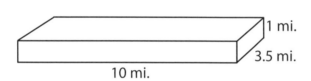

4. Volume = _____

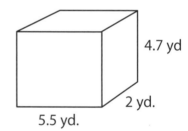

5. Volume = _____

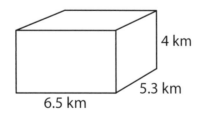

6. Volume = _____

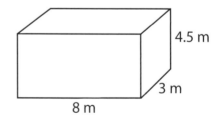

CD-104322 • © Carson-Dellosa

Labeling Lines, Line Segments, and Rays

Total Problems: **10**
Problems Correct: _____

Match the line, line segment, or ray with the correct name.

1. ← A • —— • Z →   a. $\overleftrightarrow{FM}$

2. • A ———————— • Z →   b. $\overline{FM}$

3. • F ———————— • M →   c. $\overleftrightarrow{AZ}$

4. • F ———————— • M   d. $\overline{AZ}$

5. ← • F ———— • M →   e. $\overrightarrow{AZ}$

6. • A ———————— • Z   f. $\overrightarrow{FM}$

Draw the following.

7. $\overline{JK}$

8. $\overrightarrow{HI}$

9. $\overleftrightarrow{BF}$

10. $\overleftrightarrow{VS}$

Name _____   Date _____

Naming and Measuring Angles

Name the angle and use a protractor to measure it.

Total Problems: **5**
Problems Correct: _____

1.

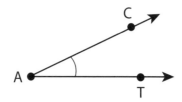

∠ _____   _____°
            angle   degree

2.

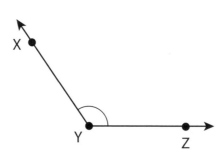

∠ _____   _____°
            angle   degree

3.

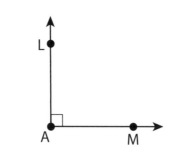

∠ _____   _____°
            angle   degree

4.

∠ _____   _____°
            angle   degree

5.

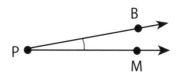

∠ _____   _____°
            angle   degree

Name _____   Date _____

Finding the Circumference of a Circle

Total Problems: 6
Problems Correct: _____

Find the circumference of each circle. Use the formula:
Circumference = π × diameter OR Circumference = π × 2 × radius.
Remember, π **= 3.14**.

1. Circumference = _____

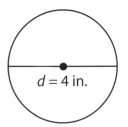

2. Circumference = _____

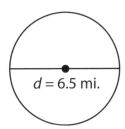

3. Circumference = _____

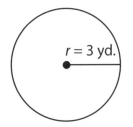

4. Circumference = _____

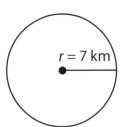

5. Circumference = _____

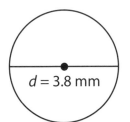

6. Circumference = _____

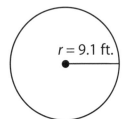

Name _____   Date _____

Labeling Bar and Circle Graphs

Total Problems: 2
Problems Correct: _____

1. **Use the information below to make a bar graph. First, name the graph. Next, name and label the *x*-axis and *y*-axis. Finally, graph the data.**

Number of pieces of trash picked up on Environment Day	
1st grade	26
2nd grade	21
3rd grade	25
4th grade	17
5th grade	22
6th grade	29

2. **Use the information below to make a circle graph. First, name the graph. Next, separate the graph into sections and label the sections according to the information provided.**

Number of students
in the school band = 16

Number of students who play
the following instruments:

Tuba, 4
Drums, 5
Flute, 2
Trumpet, 3
Clarinet, 1
Cymbals, 1

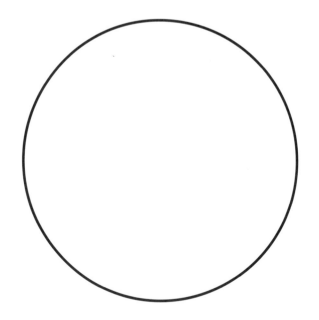

Labeling Line Graphs

Total Problems: 2
Problems Correct: _____

1. **Use the information below to make a line graph. First, name the graph. Next, name and label the *x*-axis and the *y*-axis. Finally, plot the data.**

Number of times that John went to the zoo last year	
January	1
February	3
March	2
April	4
May	2
June	5
July	7
August	4
September	1
October	4
November	3
December	2

2. **Use the information below to make a line graph. First, name the graph. Next, name and label the *x*-axis and the *y*-axis. Finally, plot the data.**

Number of times that Susan went to the park last year	
January	2
February	3
March	1
April	5
May	4
June	7
July	6
August	8
September	3
October	4
November	2
December	2

Graphing Coordinates

Total Problems: **12**
Problems Correct: _____

Graph each pair of coordinates.

1. (3, 4)
2. (1, 8)
3. (5, 1)
4. (3, 7)
5. (8, 2)
6. (6, 10)

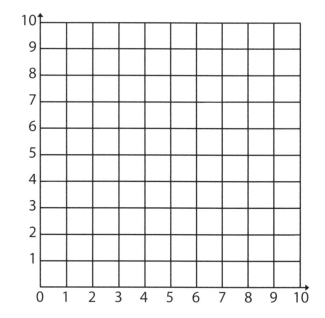

Graph each pair of coordinates.

7. (2, 9)
8. (10, 7)
9. (6, 9)
10. (1, 5)
11. (4, 3)
12. (9, 6)

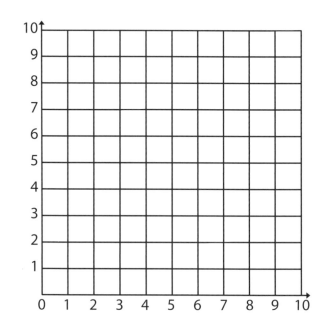

CD-104322 • © Carson-Dellosa

Graphing Coordinates

Total Problems: **12**
Problems Correct: _____

Graph each pair of coordinates.

1. (3, 5)

2. (7, 8)

3. (1, 3)

4. (6, 10)

5. (9, 4)

6. (8, 1)

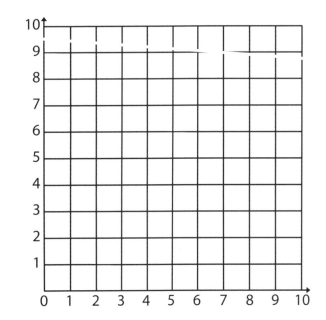

Graph each pair of coordinates.

7. (2, 6)

8. (10, 3)

9. (5, 4)

10. (7, 8)

11. (4, 10)

12. (9, 1)

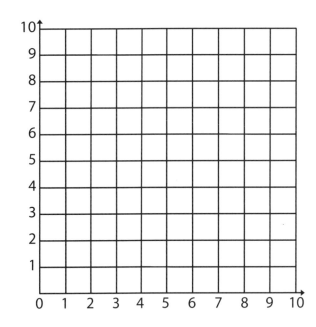

 CD-104322 • © Carson-Dellosa

Graphing Coordinates

Total Problems: **12**
Problems Correct: _____

Graph each pair of coordinates.

1. (6, 5)

2. (1, 7)

3. (10, 9)

4. (8, 3)

5. (5, 8)

6. (7, 2)

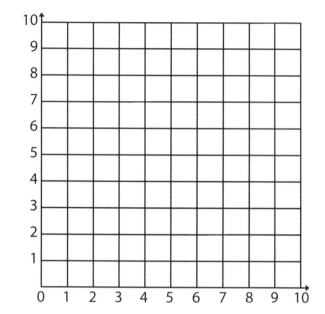

Graph each pair of coordinates.

7. (9, 5)

8. (4, 8)

9. (1, 1)

10. (6, 4)

11. (2, 6)

12. (7, 2)

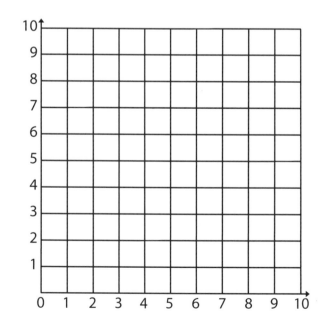

CD-104322 • © Carson-Dellosa

Number Patterns

Total Problems: **14**
Problems Correct: _____

Find the next three numbers in each number pattern.

1. 5, 8, 11, 14, 17, _____, _____, _____

2. 91, 86, 81, 76, 71, _____, _____, _____

3. 100, 92, 84, 76, 68, _____, _____, _____

4. 10, 20, 25, 35, 40, _____, _____, _____

5. 72, 69, 66, 63, 60, _____, _____, _____

6. 317, 402, 487, 572, _____, _____, _____

7. 5, 11, 23, 47, 95, _____, _____, _____

8. 244, 226, 208, 190, _____, _____, _____

9. 1, 4, 9, 16, 25, _____, _____, _____

10. 1, 2, 4, 8, 16, _____, _____, _____

11. 53, 54, 56, 59, 63, _____, _____, _____

12. 30, 34, 40, 48, 58, _____, _____, _____

13. 11, 16, 14, 19, 17, _____, _____, _____

14. 19, 34, 49, 64, 79, _____, _____, _____

Solving for Variables

Total Problems: **15**
Problems Correct: _____

Solve each equation.

1. $x + 8 = 12$

$x = 12 - 8$

$x =$ _____

2. $a - 7 = 18$

$a = 18 +$ _____

$a =$ _____

3. $z + 6 = 14$

$z = 14 -$ _____

$z =$ _____

4. $y + 8 = 11$

5. $x + 8 = 24$

6. $v + 3 = 13$

7. $m + 12 = 18$

8. $q - 15 = 100$

9. $r - 19 = 37$

10. $w - 32 = 32$

11. $z - 12 = 29$

12. $a + 7 = 20$

13. $y - 22 = 45$

14. $g + 15 = 31$

15. $n + 14 = 29$

CD-104322 • © Carson-Dellosa

Solving for Variables

Total Problems: **15**
Problems Correct: _____

Solve each equation.

1. $t \cdot 8 = 72$

$t = 72 \div 8$

$t = $ _____

2. $n \div 81 = 81$

$n = 81 \cdot$ _____

$n = $ _____

3. $y \cdot 6 = 42$

$y = 42 \div$ _____

$y = $ _____

4. $x \cdot 3 = 12$

5. $v \cdot 6 = 24$

6. $h \cdot 8 = 64$

7. $g \cdot 9 = 27$

8. $b \cdot 7 = 28$

9. $f \cdot 3 = 51$

10. $d \div 82 = 6$

11. $z \div 29 = 16$

12. $c \div 5 = 10$

13. $g \div 4 = 9$

14. $y \div 25 = 75$

15. $p \cdot 9 = 108$

Name _____ Date _____

Statistics and Probability

Total Problems: **12**
Problems Correct: _____

Use the information to determine the probability (P) of each event happening. Simplify if possible.

A jar contains 18 marbles that are all the same size. It contains 7 purple marbles, 3 green marbles, and 8 orange marbles. Without looking, Travis picks 1 marble. What is the probability of each of the following outcomes?

1. P(green) =

2. P(purple) =

3. P(orange) =

4. P(not green) =

5. P(purple or green) =

6. P(not orange) =

Use the information to determine the probability of each event happening. Simplify if possible.

A die numbered 1 through 6 is rolled. Find the probability of rolling each outcome.

7. P(5) =

8. P(1 or 2) =

9. P(odd number) =

10. P(not 6) =

11. P(even number) =

12. P(1, 2, 3, or 4) =

CD-104322 • © Carson-Dellosa

Name _____   Date _____

Mean, Median, Mode, and Range

Total Problems: **4**

Problems Correct: _____

Find the mean, median, mode, and range of each set of data.

1. 34, 41, 33, 41, 31

mean: _____

median: _____

mode: _____

range: _____

2. 18, 10. 10, 8, 35, 10, 21

mean: _____

median: _____

mode: _____

range: _____

3. 7, 14, 10, 14, 29, 16, 15

mean: _____

median: _____

mode: _____

range: _____

4. 41, 18, 24, 41, 72, 82, 16

mean: _____

median: _____

mode: _____

range: _____

Page 4

Name _____ Date _____

Adding Multi-Digit Numbers

Total Problems:	24
Problems Correct:	___

Solve each problem. Regroup when necessary.

1. 56
+ 32
88

2. 125
+ 832
957

3. 4,287
+ 907
5,194

4. 2,703
+ 9,006
11,709

5. 21,027
+ 68,509
89,536

6. 17
+ 81
98

7. 687
+ 407
1,094

8. 1,287
+ 406
1,693

9. 1,551
+ 3,287
4,838

10. 32,578
+ 10,781
43,359

11. 95
+ 59
154

12. 531
+ 450
981

13. 3,572
+ 261
3,833

14. 4,692
+ 7,841
12,533

15. 54,392
+ 62,158
116,550

16. 27
+ 42
69

17. 501
+ 225
726

18. 5,983
+ 742
6,725

19. 6,031
+ 3,275
9,306

20. 35
+ 80
115

21. 387
+ 122
509

22. 6,401
+ 578
6,979

23. 8,762
+ 5,137
13,899

24. 40,226
+ 37,822
78,048

4   CD-104322 • © Carson-Dellosa

Page 5

Name _____ Date _____

Multi-Digit Column Addition

Total Problems:	20
Problems Correct:	___

Solve each problem. Regroup when necessary.

1. 234
862
+ 335
1,431

2. 1,767
8,403
+ 2,759
12,929

3. 50,251
339
+ 42
50,632

4. 67,107
53,001
42,902
+ 107
163,117

5. 187
384
+ 416
987

6. 5,570
4,867
+ 3,210
13,647

7. 69,721
4,065
+ 13
73,799

8. 5,545
632
19
+ 45
6,241

9. 486
582
+ 23
1,091

10. 1,257
4,380
+ 9,621
15,258

11. 8,609
786
+ 52
9,447

12. 7,840
2,129
616
+ 53
10,638

13. 875
934
+ 17
1,826

14. 6,357
1,876
+ 5,072
13,305

15. 52,103
47,339
+ 857
100,299

16. 2,531
682
550
+ 49
3,812

17. 416
502
+ 22
940

18. 1,275
2,654
+ 3,023
6,952

19. 78,695
4,072
+ 3,210
85,977

20. 8,749
7,263
521
+ 84
16,617

CD-104322 • © Carson-Dellosa   5

Page 6

Name _____ Date _____

Multi-Digit Column Addition

Total Problems:	15
Problems Correct:	___

Solve each problem. Regroup when necessary.

1. 421
857
63
54
+ 7
1,402

2. 52,105
43,785
6,112
3,953
+ 4,182
110,137

3. 87,152
5,847
1,376
209
440
+ 328
95,352

4. 5,321
876
524
100
+ 76
6,897

5. 78,104
18,905
5,629
3,247
+ 432
106,317

6. 33,201
5,784
7,206
628
552
+ 16
47,387

7. 1,019
593
422
42
+ 59
2,135

8. 27,862
50,311
62,109
5,450
+ 6,219
151,951

9. 68,431
55,095
18,702
457
212
+ 12
142,909

10. 8,763
257
812
404
+ 95
10,331

11. 18,782
3,755
2,262
187
+ 555
25,541

12. 70,152
39,157
70,062
345
228
+ 12
179,956

13. 52,106
43,785
6,112
3,953
+ 4,182
110,138

14. 6,501
430
822
95
+ 42
7,890

15. 83,164
22,900
18,442
4,963
527
+ 89
130,085

6   CD-104322 • © Carson-Dellosa

Page 7

Name _____ Date _____

Subtracting One- and Two-Digit Numbers

Total Problems:	24
Problems Correct:	___

Solve each problem. Regroup when necessary.

1. 78
− 6
72

2. 25
− 7
18

3. 21
− 5
16

4. 54
− 45
9

5. 17
− 16
1

6. 56
− 4
52

7. 22
− 8
14

8. 19
− 6
13

9. 62
− 27
35

10. 95
− 67
28

11. 60
− 10
50

12. 68
− 9
59

13. 10
− 3
7

14. 85
− 67
18

15. 62
− 56
6

16. 32
− 9
23

17. 70
− 6
64

18. 71
− 4
67

19. 92
− 18
74

20. 38
− 27
11

21. 48
− 8
40

22. 84
− 7
77

23. 34
− 6
28

24. 29
− 17
12

CD-104322 • © Carson-Dellosa   7

Subtracting Two- and Three-Digit Numbers

Name _____ Date _____

Total Problems: 24
Problems Correct: _____

Solve each problem. Regroup when necessary.

1. 286 − 57 = **229**	2. 991 − 85 = **906**	3. 875 − 407 = **468**	4. 497 − 322 = **175**	5. 603 − 571 = **32**	6. 382 − 96 = **286**
7. 997 − 61 = **936**	8. 962 − 509 = **453**	9. 625 − 592 = **33**	10. 827 − 694 = **133**	11. 186 − 52 = **134**	12. 863 − 54 = **809**
13. 875 − 445 = **430**	14. 940 − 185 = **755**	15. 307 − 283 = **24**	16. 525 − 63 = **462**	17. 415 − 78 = **337**	18. 786 − 616 = **170**
19. 876 − 652 = **224**	20. 125 − 116 = **9**	21. 400 − 88 = **312**	22. 321 − 39 = **282**	23. 521 − 431 = **90**	24. 785 − 504 = **281**

Subtracting Multi-Digit Numbers

Name _____ Date _____

Total Problems: 25
Problems Correct: _____

Solve each problem. Regroup when necessary.

1. 8,907 − 52 = **8,855**	2. 4,301 − 225 = **4,076**	3. 22,107 − 3,988 = **18,119**	4. 86,946 − 71,807 = **15,139**	5. 302,175 − 68,189 = **233,986**
6. 6,217 − 25 = **6,192**	7. 5,681 − 309 = **5,372**	8. 31,257 − 4,071 = **27,186**	9. 47,810 − 22,516 = **25,294**	10. 496,502 − 10,498 = **486,004**
11. 8,357 − 78 = **8,279**	12. 7,662 − 447 = **7,215**	13. 46,689 − 5,672 = **41,017**	14. 25,300 − 18,704 = **6,596**	15. 187,645 − 53,217 = **134,428**
16. 1,358 − 32 = **1,326**	17. 5,432 − 151 = **5,281**	18. 76,571 − 6,229 = **70,342**	19. 6,219 − 52 = **6,167**	20. 8,719 − 582 = **8,137**
21. 52,398 − 1,028 = **51,370**	22. 86,107 − 83,279 = **2,828**	23. 36,875 − 31,787 = **5,088**	24. 63,128 − 57,281 = **5,847**	25. 94,422 − 5,349 = **89,073**

Multiplying One- and Two-Digit Numbers

Name _____ Date _____

Total Problems: 30
Problems Correct: _____

Solve each problem. Regroup when necessary.

1. 6 × 9 = **54**	2. 5 × 3 = **15**	3. 11 × 4 = **44**	4. 12 × 5 = **60**	5. 9 × 3 = **27**	6. 4 × 7 = **28**
7. 10 × 3 = **30**	8. 8 × 8 = **64**	9. 10 × 4 = **40**	10. 7 × 8 = **56**	11. 8 × 9 = **72**	12. 5 × 8 = **40**
13. 5 × 5 = **25**	14. 12 × 12 = **144**	15. 4 × 5 = **20**	16. 11 × 2 = **22**	17. 11 × 10 = **110**	18. 12 × 4 = **48**
19. 11 × 9 = **99**	20. 7 × 9 = **63**	21. 10 × 10 = **100**	22. 10 × 9 = **90**	23. 10 × 8 = **80**	24. 11 × 8 = **88**
25. 4 × 3 = **12**	26. 5 × 7 = **35**	27. 9 × 6 = **54**	28. 11 × 12 = **132**	29. 6 × 3 = **18**	30. 6 × 6 = **36**

Multiplying Two-Digit Numbers

Name _____ Date _____

Total Problems: 20
Problems Correct: _____

Solve each problem. Regroup when necessary.

1. 27 × 13 = **351**	2. 15 × 47 = **705**	3. 84 × 19 = **1,596**	4. 58 × 61 = **3,538**	5. 45 × 62 = **2,790**
6. 87 × 93 = **8,091**	7. 22 × 38 = **836**	8. 82 × 27 = **2,214**	9. 33 × 51 = **1,683**	10. 46 × 41 = **1,886**
11. 47 × 25 = **1,175**	12. 24 × 43 = **1,032**	13. 42 × 51 = **2,142**	14. 87 × 65 = **5,655**	15. 48 × 62 = **2,976**
16. 68 × 59 = **4,012**	17. 65 × 92 = **5,980**	18. 23 × 50 = **1,150**	19. 83 × 60 = **4,980**	20. 72 × 57 = **4,104**

Page 12

Name _____ Date _____

Multiplying Multi-Digit Numbers

Solve each problem. Regroup when necessary.

Total Problems: 24
Problems Correct: _____

1.	2.	3.	4.	5.	6.
87 $\times$ 5	72 $\times$ 18	425 $\times$ 15	303 $\times$ 83	187 $\times$ 26	93 $\times$ 6
435	**1,296**	**6,375**	**25,149**	**4,862**	**558**

7.	8.	9.	10.	11.	12.
63 $\times$ 25	313 $\times$ 72	442 $\times$ 81	593 $\times$ 45	84 $\times$ 3	42 $\times$ 28
1,575	**22,536**	**35,802**	**26,685**	**252**	**1,176**

13.	14.	15.	16.	17.	18.
81 $\times$ 53	872 $\times$ 20	351 $\times$ 67	52 $\times$ 4	75 $\times$ 21	21 $\times$ 10
4,293	**17,440**	**23,517**	**208**	**1,575**	**210**

19.	20.	21.	22.	23.	24.
214 $\times$ 87	109 $\times$ 15	12 $\times$ 9	16 $\times$ 8	87 $\times$ 26	99 $\times$ 21
18,618	**1,635**	**108**	**128**	**2,262**	**2,079**

12 CD-104322 • © Carson-Dellosa

Page 13

Name _____ Date _____

Multiplying Multi-Digit Numbers

Solve each problem. Regroup when necessary.

Total Problems: 20
Problems Correct: _____

1.	2.	3.	4.	5.
918 $\times$ 55	755 $\times$ 221	618 $\times$ 500	1,242 $\times$ 687	437 $\times$ 22
50,490	**166,855**	**309,000**	**853,254**	**9,614**

6.	7.	8.	9.	10.
832 $\times$ 106	391 $\times$ 125	3,861 $\times$ 392	518 $\times$ 42	391 $\times$ 535
88,192	**48,875**	**1,513,512**	**21,756**	**209,185**

11.	12.	13.	14.	15.
482 $\times$ 663	4,369 $\times$ 873	925 $\times$ 54	851 $\times$ 462	331 $\times$ 528
319,566	**3,814,137**	**49,950**	**393,162**	**174,768**

16.	17.	18.	19.	20.
7,421 $\times$ 694	622 $\times$ 33	795 $\times$ 787	435 $\times$ 683	5,872 $\times$ 515
5,150,174	**20,526**	**625,665**	**297,105**	**3,024,080**

CD-104322 • © Carson-Dellosa 13

Page 14

Name _____ Date _____

Division with One-Digit Quotients

Solve each problem.

Total Problems: 24
Problems Correct: _____

1. $8\overline{)64}$ = **8**	2. $5\overline{)25}$ = **5**	3. $6\overline{)30}$ = **5**
4. $5\overline{)40}$ = **8**	5. $4\overline{)20}$ = **5**	6. $9\overline{)81}$ = **9**
7. $8\overline{)24}$ = **3**	8. $7\overline{)77}$ = **11**	9. $8\overline{)32}$ = **4**
10. $9\overline{)27}$ = **3**	11. $7\overline{)42}$ = **6**	12. $6\overline{)54}$ = **9**
13. $6\overline{)36}$ = **6**	14. $3\overline{)12}$ = **4**	15. $5\overline{)30}$ = **6**
16. $8\overline{)56}$ = **7**	17. $8\overline{)16}$ = **2**	18. $5\overline{)35}$ = **7**
19. $7\overline{)14}$ = **2**	20. $9\overline{)36}$ = **4**	21. $6\overline{)24}$ = **4**
22. $9\overline{)90}$ = **10**	23. $9\overline{)63}$ = **7**	24. $6\overline{)60}$ = **10**

14 CD-104322 • © Carson-Dellosa

Page 15

Name _____ Date _____

Division with One-Digit Quotients

Solve each problem.

Total Problems: 20
Problems Correct: _____

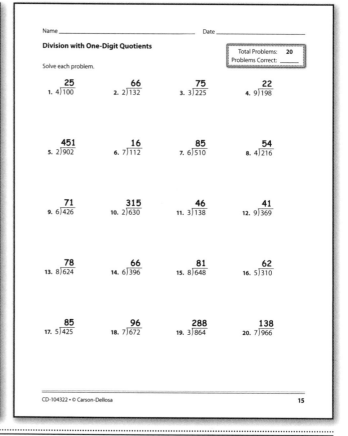

1. $4\overline{)100}$ = **25**	2. $2\overline{)132}$ = **66**	3. $3\overline{)225}$ = **75**	4. $9\overline{)198}$ = **22**
5. $2\overline{)902}$ = **451**	6. $7\overline{)112}$ = **16**	7. $6\overline{)510}$ = **85**	8. $4\overline{)216}$ = **54**
9. $6\overline{)426}$ = **71**	10. $2\overline{)630}$ = **315**	11. $3\overline{)138}$ = **46**	12. $9\overline{)369}$ = **41**
13. $8\overline{)624}$ = **78**	14. $6\overline{)396}$ = **66**	15. $8\overline{)648}$ = **81**	16. $5\overline{)310}$ = **62**
17. $5\overline{)425}$ = **85**	18. $7\overline{)672}$ = **96**	19. $3\overline{)864}$ = **288**	20. $7\overline{)966}$ = **138**

CD-104322 • © Carson-Dellosa 15

Worksheet 1 (page 16)

Name _____ Date _____

Division with Two-Digit Quotients

Total Problems: 20
Problems Correct: _____

Solve each problem.

1. 14 — 22)308
2. 18 — 17)306
3. 50 — 24)1,200
4. 55 — 86)4,730

5. 61 — 73)4,453
6. 26 — 11)286
7. 29 — 33)957
8. 28 — 38)1,064

9. 52 — 74)3,848
10. 62 — 29)1,798
11. 52 — 16)832
12. 17 — 53)901

13. 33 — 45)1,485
14. 56 — 91)5,096
15. 24 — 82)1,968
16. 14 — 41)574

17. 12 — 62)744
18. 63 — 57)3,591
19. 72 — 18)1,296
20. 42 — 95)3,990

16   CD-104322 • © Carson-Dellosa

Worksheet 2 (page 17)

Name _____ Date _____

Division with One- and Two-Digit Quotients and Remainders

Total Problems: 20
Problems Correct: _____

Solve each problem.

1. 9 r3 — 8)75
2. 4 r11 — 24)107
3. 11 r13 — 48)541
4. 26 r4 — 18)472

5. 23 r8 — 22)514
6. 16 r3 — 4)67
7. 28 r3 — 16)451
8. 12 r10 — 62)754

9. 29 r18 — 23)685
10. 16 r12 — 42)684
11. 11 r2 — 6)68
12. 5 r27 — 32)187

13. 41 r8 — 13)541
14. 20 r11 — 46)931
15. 6 r3 — 52)315
16. 26 r1 — 3)79

17. 16 r7 — 51)823
18. 11 r51 — 72)843
19. 13 r7 — 50)657
20. 15 r7 — 37)562

CD-104322 • © Carson-Dellosa   17

Worksheet 3 (page 18)

Name _____ Date _____

Division with Two- and Three-Digit Quotients and Remainders

Total Problems: 20
Problems Correct: _____

Solve each problem.

1. 56 r2 — 28)1,570
2. 127 r15 — 36)4,587
3. 120 r38 — 81)9,758
4. 11 r227 — 561)6,398

5. 52 r43 — 122)6,387
6. 134 r10 — 16)2,154
7. 19 r20 — 97)1,863
8. 199 r5 — 19)3,786

9. 21 r116 — 117)2,573
10. 13 r122 — 184)2,514
11. 106 r42 — 47)5,024
12. 117 r36 — 65)7,641

13. 191 r13 — 24)4,597
14. 19 r203 — 264)5,219
15. 8 r191 — 512)4,287
16. 85 r18 — 53)4,523

17. 124 r14 — 72)8,942
18. 112 r8 — 38)4,264
19. 20 r8 — 435)8,708
20. 18 r59 — 371)6,737

18   CD-104322 • © Carson-Dellosa

Worksheet 4 (page 19)

Name _____ Date _____

Understanding Fractions

Total Problems: 12
Problems Correct: _____

Write the fraction for each of the following descriptions.

1. four-fifths $\frac{4}{5}$
2. two-thirds $\frac{2}{3}$

3. three-eighths $\frac{3}{8}$
4. Numerator 1, Denominator 10 $\frac{1}{10}$

5. Denominator 7, Numerator 9 $\frac{9}{7}$
6. Numerator 3, Denominator 4 $\frac{3}{4}$

Shade each shape to show the fraction.

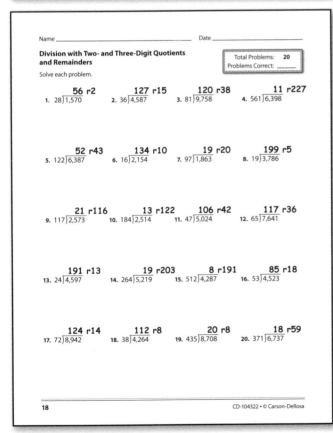

7. $\frac{5}{6}$
8. $\frac{3}{4}$
9. $\frac{1}{5}$

Draw lines to divide each shape. Then, shade each shape to show the fraction.

10. $\frac{1}{2}$
11. $\frac{9}{10}$
12. $\frac{7}{8}$

CD-104322 • © Carson-Dellosa   19

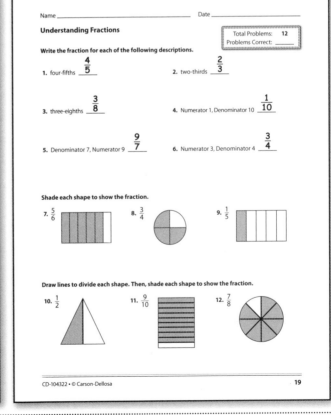

Making Fractions Equivalent

Name _____ Date _____

Total Problems: 20
Problems Correct: _____

Make each pair of fractions equivalent.

1. $\frac{1}{2} = \frac{2}{4}$ 2. $\frac{3}{5} = \frac{12}{20}$ 3. $\frac{5}{6} = \frac{35}{42}$ 4. $\frac{3}{4} = \frac{9}{12}$

5. $\frac{2}{3} = \frac{8}{12}$ 6. $\frac{1}{5} = \frac{5}{25}$ 7. $\frac{1}{4} = \frac{2}{8}$ 8. $\frac{2}{7} = \frac{4}{14}$

9. $\frac{3}{7} = \frac{12}{28}$ 10. $\frac{1}{3} = \frac{3}{9}$ 11. $\frac{2}{3} = \frac{10}{15}$ 12. $\frac{1}{8} = \frac{8}{64}$

13. $\frac{2}{5} = \frac{6}{15}$ 14. $\frac{3}{4} = \frac{9}{12}$ 15. $\frac{6}{7} = \frac{12}{14}$ 16. $\frac{4}{5} = \frac{12}{15}$

Fill in the numbers to complete each row, making each fraction equivalent to the first one.

17. $\frac{1}{2} = \frac{3}{6} = \frac{4}{8} = \frac{6}{12} = \frac{2}{4} = \frac{5}{10}$

18. $\frac{2}{3} = \frac{8}{12} = \frac{4}{6} = \frac{10}{15} = \frac{6}{9} = \frac{12}{18}$

19. $\frac{1}{4} = \frac{2}{8} = \frac{5}{20} = \frac{3}{12} = \frac{6}{24} = \frac{4}{16}$

20. $\frac{3}{5} = \frac{15}{25} = \frac{9}{15} = \frac{6}{10} = \frac{12}{20} = \frac{18}{30}$

20

Comparing Fractions

Name _____ Date _____

Total Problems: 15
Problems Correct: _____

Write >, <, or = to make each statement true.

1. $\frac{1}{2}$ ⊜ $\frac{4}{8}$ 2. $\frac{2}{5}$ ⊛ $\frac{3}{4}$ 3. $\frac{5}{6}$ ⊛ $\frac{7}{8}$

4. $\frac{5}{8}$ ⊛ $\frac{13}{32}$ 5. $\frac{1}{8}$ ⊛ $\frac{3}{5}$ 6. $\frac{1}{4}$ ⊛ $\frac{2}{3}$

7. $\frac{1}{6}$ ⊛ $\frac{1}{3}$ 8. $\frac{4}{5}$ ⊜ $\frac{16}{20}$ 9. $\frac{2}{3}$ ⊛ $\frac{1}{5}$

10. $\frac{1}{2}$ ⊛ $\frac{4}{5}$ 11. $\frac{11}{16}$ ⊛ $\frac{3}{8}$ 12. $\frac{4}{7}$ ⊛ $\frac{1}{2}$

Rewrite each series of fractions so that they have like denominators. Order each series from smallest to largest. Then, write each fraction in simplest form.

	Same denominator, smallest to largest	Simplest form
13. $\frac{1}{3}, \frac{3}{4}, \frac{1}{2}$	$\frac{4}{12}$ $\frac{6}{12}$ $\frac{9}{12}$	$\frac{1}{3}$ $\frac{1}{2}$ $\frac{3}{4}$
14. $\frac{5}{6}, \frac{2}{9}, \frac{1}{3}$	$\frac{8}{36}$ $\frac{12}{36}$ $\frac{30}{36}$	$\frac{2}{9}$ $\frac{1}{3}$ $\frac{5}{6}$
15. $\frac{1}{6}, \frac{7}{8}, \frac{3}{4}$	$\frac{4}{24}$ $\frac{18}{24}$ $\frac{21}{24}$	$\frac{1}{6}$ $\frac{3}{4}$ $\frac{7}{8}$

21

Finding the Greatest Common Factor

Name _____ Date _____

Total Problems: 10
Problems Correct: _____

List the common factors of the numerator and denominator of each fraction. Then, write the greatest common factor (GCF). Divide the numerator and denominator by the GCF and write each fraction in simplest form.

	Fraction	Common Factors	GCF	Simplest Form
1.	$\frac{10}{12}$	1, 2	2	$\frac{5}{6}$
2.	$\frac{18}{27}$	1, 3, 9	9	$\frac{2}{3}$
3.	$\frac{25}{100}$	1, 5, 25	25	$\frac{1}{4}$
4.	$\frac{5}{30}$	1, 5	5	$\frac{1}{6}$
5.	$\frac{12}{30}$	1, 2, 3, 6	6	$\frac{2}{5}$
6.	$\frac{24}{32}$	1, 2, 4, 8	8	$\frac{3}{4}$
7.	$\frac{14}{21}$	1, 7	7	$\frac{2}{3}$
8.	$\frac{8}{40}$	1, 2, 4, 8	8	$\frac{1}{5}$
9.	$\frac{15}{18}$	1, 3	3	$\frac{5}{6}$
10.	$\frac{10}{20}$	1, 2, 5, 10	10	$\frac{1}{2}$

22

Writing Fractions in Simplest Form

Name _____ Date _____

Total Problems: 24
Problems Correct: _____

Write each fraction or mixed number in simplest form.

1. $\frac{6}{8} = \frac{3}{4}$ 2. $\frac{6}{15} = \frac{2}{5}$ 3. $\frac{27}{81} = \frac{1}{3}$

4. $2\frac{24}{30} = 2\frac{4}{5}$ 5. $4\frac{4}{8} = 4\frac{1}{2}$ 6. $\frac{2}{4} = \frac{1}{2}$

7. $\frac{2}{10} = \frac{1}{5}$ 8. $\frac{12}{24} = \frac{1}{2}$ 9. $3\frac{12}{18} = 3\frac{2}{3}$

10. $5\frac{10}{15} = 5\frac{2}{3}$ 11. $\frac{15}{18} = \frac{5}{6}$ 12. $\frac{20}{40} = \frac{1}{2}$

13. $\frac{10}{15} = \frac{2}{3}$ 14. $1\frac{18}{20} = 1\frac{9}{10}$ 15. $3\frac{6}{9} = 3\frac{2}{3}$

16. $\frac{16}{24} = \frac{2}{3}$ 17. $\frac{16}{32} = \frac{1}{2}$ 18. $\frac{14}{21} = \frac{2}{3}$

19. $4\frac{3}{24} = 4\frac{1}{8}$ 20. $2\frac{8}{32} = 2\frac{1}{4}$ 21. $\frac{10}{40} = \frac{1}{4}$

22. $\frac{56}{64} = \frac{7}{8}$ 23. $3\frac{6}{18} = 3\frac{1}{3}$ 24. $\frac{48}{50} = \frac{24}{25}$

23

Name _____ Date _____

Writing Mixed Numbers as Improper Fractions

Total Problems:	10
Problems Correct:	_____

Write each mixed number as an improper fraction.

1. $2\frac{3}{4} = \frac{(2 \times 4) + 3}{4} = \frac{11}{4}$

2. $3\frac{1}{3} = \frac{(3 \times 1) + 3}{3} = \frac{10}{3}$

3. $2\frac{7}{8} = \frac{(2 \times 8) + 7}{8} = \frac{23}{8}$

4. $7\frac{3}{4} = \frac{(7 \times 4) + 3}{4} = \frac{31}{4}$

5. $1\frac{4}{5} = \frac{(1 \times 5) + 4}{5} = \frac{9}{5}$

6. $4\frac{3}{8} = \frac{(4 \times 8) + 3}{8} = \frac{35}{8}$

7. $1\frac{2}{5} = \frac{(1 \times 5) + 2}{5} = \frac{7}{5}$

8. $4\frac{5}{6} = \frac{(4 \times 6) + 5}{6} = \frac{29}{6}$

9. $2\frac{7}{9} = \frac{(2 \times 9) + 7}{9} = \frac{25}{9}$

10. $5\frac{3}{11} = \frac{(5 \times 11) + 3}{11} = \frac{58}{11}$

Name _____ Date _____

Writing Mixed Numbers as Improper Fractions

Total Problems:	12
Problems Correct:	_____

Write each mixed number as an improper fraction.

1. $2\frac{5}{8} = \frac{21}{8}$

2. $3\frac{6}{7} = \frac{27}{7}$

3. $8\frac{5}{11} = \frac{93}{11}$

4. $8\frac{2}{3} = \frac{26}{3}$

5. $4\frac{1}{2} = \frac{9}{2}$

6. $8\frac{7}{8} = \frac{71}{8}$

7. $3\frac{3}{10} = \frac{33}{10}$

8. $2\frac{3}{5} = \frac{13}{5}$

9. $6\frac{3}{4} = \frac{27}{4}$

10. $2\frac{1}{9} = \frac{19}{9}$

11. $4\frac{5}{12} = \frac{53}{5}$

12. $5\frac{5}{7} = \frac{40}{7}$

Name _____ Date _____

Writing Improper Fractions as Mixed Numbers

Total Problems:	10
Problems Correct:	_____

Write each improper fraction as a mixed number.

1. $\frac{15}{8} = 8\overline{)15} = 1\frac{7}{8}$

2. $\frac{25}{13} = 13\overline{)25} = 1\frac{12}{13}$

3. $\frac{54}{7} = 7\overline{)54} = 7\frac{5}{7}$

4. $\frac{29}{5} = 5\overline{)29} = 5\frac{4}{5}$

5. $\frac{85}{22} = 22\overline{)85} = 3\frac{19}{22}$

6. $\frac{10}{4} = 4\overline{)10} = 2\frac{1}{2}$

7. $\frac{62}{8} = 8\overline{)62} = 7\frac{3}{4}$

8. $\frac{34}{10} = 10\overline{)34} = 3\frac{2}{5}$

9. $\frac{43}{16} = 16\overline{)43} = 2\frac{11}{16}$

10. $\frac{33}{7} = 7\overline{)33} = 4\frac{5}{7}$

Name _____ Date _____

Writing Improper Fractions as Mixed Numbers

Total Problems:	10
Problems Correct:	_____

Write each improper fraction as a mixed number.

1. $\frac{16}{7} = 2\frac{2}{7}$

2. $\frac{32}{9} = 3\frac{5}{9}$

3. $\frac{37}{12} = 3\frac{1}{12}$

4. $\frac{12}{5} = 2\frac{2}{5}$

5. $\frac{50}{27} = 1\frac{23}{27}$

6. $\frac{10}{4} = 2\frac{1}{2}$

7. $\frac{53}{16} = 3\frac{5}{16}$

8. $\frac{86}{19} = 4\frac{10}{19}$

9. $\frac{14}{13} = 1\frac{1}{13}$

10. $\frac{43}{20} = 2\frac{3}{20}$

Worksheet 1 (page 28)

Name _____ Date _____

Fractions Review

Total Problems: 25
Problems Correct: _____

Make each pair of fractions equivalent.

1. $\frac{3}{4} = \frac{12}{16}$　　2. $\frac{5}{6} = \frac{25}{30}$　　3. $\frac{3}{8} = \frac{12}{32}$

4. $\frac{1}{3} = \frac{3}{9}$　　5. $\frac{5}{12} = \frac{25}{60}$　　6. $\frac{1}{5} = \frac{5}{25}$

Write <, >, or = to make each statement true.

7. $3 \gt \frac{6}{5}$　　8. $\frac{7}{9} \gt \frac{5}{18}$　　9. $\frac{3}{4} \gt \frac{2}{3}$

10. $\frac{1}{2} \gt \frac{1}{3}$　　11. $\frac{12}{24} = \frac{1}{2}$　　12. $\frac{7}{8} \gt \frac{7}{16}$

List the common factors of the numerator and denominator of each fraction. Then, write the GCF. Divide the numerator and denominator by the GCF and write each fraction in simplest form.

	Fraction	Common Factors	GCF	Simplest Form
13.	$\frac{12}{24}$	1,2,3,4,6,12	12	$\frac{1}{2}$
14.	$\frac{21}{28}$	1,7	7	$\frac{3}{4}$
15.	$\frac{16}{32}$	1,2,4,8,16	16	$\frac{1}{2}$
16.	$\frac{45}{54}$	1,3,9	9	$\frac{5}{6}$

Write each improper fraction as a mixed number.

17. $\frac{25}{15} = 1\frac{2}{3}$　　18. $\frac{43}{16} = 2\frac{9}{16}$　　19. $\frac{64}{10} = 6\frac{2}{5}$

20. $\frac{30}{14} = 2\frac{1}{7}$　　21. $\frac{32}{9} = 3\frac{5}{9}$　　22. $\frac{10}{8} = 1\frac{1}{4}$

23. $\frac{12}{7} = 1\frac{5}{7}$　　24. $\frac{16}{12} = 1\frac{1}{3}$　　25. $\frac{14}{3} = 4\frac{2}{3}$

28　　CD-104322 • © Carson-Dellosa

Worksheet 2 (page 29)

Name _____ Date _____

Finding the Least Common Denominator

Total Problems: 12
Problems Correct: _____

Find the least common denominator (LCD) for each pair of fractions.

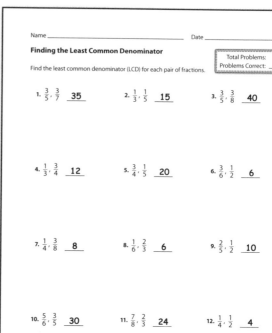

1. $\frac{3}{5}, \frac{3}{7}$　__35__　　2. $\frac{1}{3}, \frac{1}{5}$　__15__　　3. $\frac{3}{5}, \frac{3}{8}$　__40__

4. $\frac{1}{3}, \frac{3}{4}$　__12__　　5. $\frac{3}{4}, \frac{1}{5}$　__20__　　6. $\frac{3}{6}, \frac{1}{2}$　__6__

7. $\frac{1}{4}, \frac{3}{8}$　__8__　　8. $\frac{1}{6}, \frac{2}{3}$　__6__　　9. $\frac{2}{5}, \frac{1}{2}$　__10__

10. $\frac{5}{6}, \frac{3}{5}$　__30__　　11. $\frac{7}{8}, \frac{2}{3}$　__24__　　12. $\frac{1}{4}, \frac{1}{2}$　__4__

CD-104322 • © Carson-Dellosa　　29

Worksheet 3 (page 30)

Name _____ Date _____

Adding Fractions with Like Denominators

Total Problems: 15
Problems Correct: _____

Solve each problem. Write each answer in simplest form.

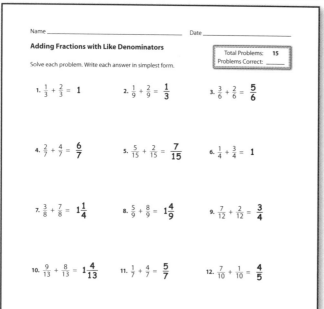

1. $\frac{1}{3} + \frac{2}{3} = 1$　　2. $\frac{1}{9} + \frac{2}{9} = \frac{1}{3}$　　3. $\frac{3}{6} + \frac{2}{6} = \frac{5}{6}$

4. $\frac{2}{7} + \frac{4}{7} = \frac{6}{7}$　　5. $\frac{5}{15} + \frac{2}{15} = \frac{7}{15}$　　6. $\frac{1}{4} + \frac{3}{4} = 1$

7. $\frac{3}{8} + \frac{7}{8} = 1\frac{1}{4}$　　8. $\frac{5}{9} + \frac{8}{9} = 1\frac{4}{9}$　　9. $\frac{7}{12} + \frac{2}{12} = \frac{3}{4}$

10. $\frac{9}{13} + \frac{8}{13} = 1\frac{4}{13}$　　11. $\frac{1}{7} + \frac{4}{7} = \frac{5}{7}$　　12. $\frac{7}{10} + \frac{1}{10} = \frac{4}{5}$

13. $\frac{1}{2} + \frac{1}{2} = 1$　　14. $\frac{2}{5} + \frac{5}{5} = 1\frac{2}{5}$　　15. $\frac{4}{12} + \frac{3}{12} = \frac{7}{12}$

30　　CD-104322 • © Carson-Dellosa

Worksheet 4 (page 31)

Name _____ Date _____

Adding Fractions with Like Denominators

Total Problems: 16
Problems Correct: _____

Solve each problem. Write each answer in simplest form.

1. $\begin{array}{r} \frac{4}{9} \\ + \frac{2}{9} \\ \hline \frac{2}{3} \end{array}$　　2. $\begin{array}{r} \frac{5}{6} \\ + \frac{1}{6} \\ \hline 1 \end{array}$　　3. $\begin{array}{r} \frac{5}{8} \\ + \frac{1}{8} \\ \hline \frac{3}{4} \end{array}$　　4. $\begin{array}{r} \frac{4}{5} \\ + \frac{2}{5} \\ \hline 1\frac{1}{5} \end{array}$

5. $\begin{array}{r} \frac{1}{5} \\ + \frac{2}{5} \\ \hline \frac{3}{5} \end{array}$　　6. $\begin{array}{r} \frac{3}{7} \\ + \frac{1}{7} \\ \hline \frac{4}{7} \end{array}$　　7. $\begin{array}{r} \frac{1}{3} \\ + \frac{1}{3} \\ \hline \frac{2}{3} \end{array}$　　8. $\begin{array}{r} \frac{10}{13} \\ + \frac{11}{13} \\ \hline 1\frac{8}{13} \end{array}$

9. $\begin{array}{r} \frac{7}{12} \\ + \frac{5}{12} \\ \hline 1 \end{array}$　　10. $\begin{array}{r} \frac{2}{15} \\ + \frac{3}{15} \\ \hline \frac{1}{3} \end{array}$　　11. $\begin{array}{r} \frac{2}{17} \\ + \frac{4}{17} \\ \hline \frac{6}{17} \end{array}$　　12. $\begin{array}{r} \frac{5}{18} \\ + \frac{3}{18} \\ \hline \frac{4}{9} \end{array}$

13. $\begin{array}{r} \frac{7}{10} \\ + \frac{7}{10} \\ \hline 1\frac{2}{5} \end{array}$　　14. $\begin{array}{r} \frac{9}{11} \\ + \frac{6}{11} \\ \hline 1\frac{4}{11} \end{array}$　　15. $\begin{array}{r} \frac{4}{10} \\ + \frac{2}{10} \\ \hline \frac{3}{5} \end{array}$　　16. $\begin{array}{r} \frac{1}{2} \\ + \frac{1}{2} \\ \hline 1 \end{array}$

CD-104322 • © Carson-Dellosa　　31

Name _____ Date _____

Adding Fractions with Unlike Denominators

Total Problems: 15
Problems Correct: _____

Solve each problem. Write each answer in simplest form.

1. $\frac{1}{2} + \frac{2}{5} = \frac{9}{10}$　　2. $\frac{1}{6} + \frac{3}{4} = \frac{11}{12}$　　3. $\frac{1}{8} + \frac{3}{4} = \frac{7}{8}$

4. $\frac{2}{3} + \frac{3}{4} = 1\frac{5}{12}$　　5. $\frac{5}{12} + \frac{2}{10} = \frac{37}{60}$　　6. $\frac{2}{3} + \frac{3}{5} = 1\frac{4}{15}$

7. $\frac{3}{7} + \frac{1}{3} = \frac{16}{21}$　　8. $\frac{1}{9} + \frac{2}{7} = \frac{25}{63}$　　9. $\frac{7}{10} + \frac{3}{12} = \frac{19}{20}$

10. $\frac{1}{6} + \frac{3}{5} = \frac{23}{30}$　　11. $\frac{1}{4} + \frac{3}{8} = \frac{5}{8}$　　12. $\frac{1}{10} + \frac{2}{11} = \frac{31}{110}$

13. $\frac{2}{5} + \frac{1}{3} = \frac{11}{15}$　　14. $\frac{2}{7} + \frac{5}{6} = 1\frac{5}{42}$　　15. $\frac{3}{5} + \frac{1}{10} = \frac{7}{10}$

CD-104322 • © Carson-Dellosa

Name _____ Date _____

Adding Fractions with Unlike Denominators

Total Problems: 15
Problems Correct: _____

Solve each problem. Write each answer in simplest form.

1. $\frac{1}{4} + \frac{3}{5} = \frac{17}{20}$

2. $\frac{1}{2} + \frac{1}{5} = \frac{7}{10}$

3. $\frac{4}{5} + \frac{2}{3} = 1\frac{7}{15}$

4. $\frac{2}{3} + \frac{2}{5} = 1\frac{1}{15}$

5. $\frac{4}{5} + \frac{7}{8} = 1\frac{27}{40}$

6. $\frac{3}{4} + \frac{1}{3} = 1\frac{1}{12}$

7. $\frac{1}{6} + \frac{3}{5} = \frac{17}{30}$

8. $\frac{3}{6} + \frac{3}{4} = 1\frac{1}{4}$

9. $\frac{1}{4} + \frac{2}{3} = \frac{11}{12}$

10. $\frac{5}{8} + \frac{2}{3} = 1\frac{7}{24}$

11. $\frac{2}{5} + \frac{1}{3} = \frac{11}{15}$

12. $\frac{1}{3} + \frac{5}{7} = 1\frac{1}{21}$

13. $\frac{1}{4} + \frac{7}{8} = 1\frac{1}{8}$

14. $\frac{2}{3} + \frac{2}{10} = \frac{13}{15}$

15. $\frac{1}{3} + \frac{2}{6} = \frac{2}{3}$

CD-104322 • © Carson-Dellosa　

Name _____ Date _____

Adding Mixed Numbers with Like Denominators

Total Problems: 12
Problems Correct: _____

Solve each problem. Write each answer in simplest form.

1. $3\frac{1}{4} + 2\frac{2}{4} = 5\frac{3}{4}$　　2. $5\frac{1}{3} + 2\frac{1}{3} = 7\frac{2}{3}$　　3. $5\frac{8}{9} + 6\frac{2}{9} = 12\frac{1}{9}$

4. $5\frac{1}{8} + 6\frac{5}{8} = 11\frac{3}{4}$　　5. $5\frac{1}{8} + 2\frac{3}{8} = 7\frac{1}{2}$　　6. $3\frac{1}{6} + 2\frac{1}{6} = 5\frac{1}{3}$

7. $4\frac{4}{5} + 3\frac{3}{5} = 8\frac{2}{5}$　　8. $4\frac{1}{3} + 5\frac{2}{3} = 10$　　9. $7\frac{2}{9} + 1\frac{5}{9} = 8\frac{7}{9}$

10. $2\frac{2}{5} + 1\frac{3}{5} = 4$　　11. $2\frac{5}{7} + 3\frac{6}{7} = 6\frac{4}{7}$　　12. $7\frac{5}{6} + 8\frac{4}{6} = 16\frac{1}{2}$

CD-104322 • © Carson-Dellosa

Name _____ Date _____

Adding Mixed Numbers with Like Denominators

Total Problems: 14
Problems Correct: _____

Solve each problem. Write each answer in simplest form.

1. $1\frac{6}{8} + 2\frac{4}{8} = 4\frac{1}{4}$　　2. $3\frac{2}{6} + 4\frac{3}{6} = 7\frac{5}{6}$

3. $5\frac{5}{16} + 3\frac{7}{16} = 8\frac{3}{4}$　　4. $3\frac{1}{4} + 6\frac{1}{4} = 9\frac{1}{2}$

5. $8\frac{1}{6} + 4\frac{5}{6} = 13$　　6. $3\frac{3}{7} + 4\frac{3}{7} = 7\frac{6}{7}$

7. $8\frac{5}{6} + 7\frac{5}{6} = 16\frac{2}{3}$　　8. $7\frac{1}{3} + 7\frac{2}{3} = 15$

9. $5\frac{3}{8} + 4\frac{1}{8} = 9\frac{1}{2}$　　10. $3\frac{9}{10} + 2\frac{7}{10} = 6\frac{3}{5}$　　11. $1\frac{5}{12} + 7\frac{11}{12} = 9\frac{1}{3}$

12. $2\frac{7}{9} + 5\frac{4}{9} = 8\frac{2}{9}$　　13. $7\frac{4}{5} + 3\frac{1}{5} = 11$　　14. $4\frac{2}{3} + 6\frac{2}{3} = 11\frac{1}{3}$

CD-104322 • © Carson-Dellosa　

Page 36

Name _____ Date _____

Adding Mixed Numbers with Unlike Denominators

Total Problems:	15
Problems Correct:	_____

Solve each problem. Write each answer in simplest form.

1. $4\frac{1}{8} + 5\frac{3}{4} = \mathbf{9\frac{7}{8}}$ 2. $4\frac{7}{8} + 6\frac{1}{4} = \mathbf{11\frac{1}{8}}$ 3. $4\frac{3}{4} + 1\frac{2}{3} = \mathbf{6\frac{5}{12}}$

4. $4\frac{1}{8} + 5\frac{1}{5} = \mathbf{9\frac{13}{40}}$ 5. $8\frac{3}{4} + 7\frac{3}{16} = \mathbf{15\frac{15}{16}}$ 6. $6\frac{1}{2} + 6\frac{2}{5} = \mathbf{12\frac{9}{10}}$

7. $8\frac{1}{3} + 2\frac{3}{7} = \mathbf{10\frac{16}{21}}$ 8. $5\frac{1}{8} + 6\frac{2}{5} = \mathbf{11\frac{21}{40}}$ 9. $1\frac{9}{10} + 3\frac{1}{4} = \mathbf{5\frac{3}{20}}$

10. $2\frac{3}{4} + 3\frac{5}{6} = \mathbf{6\frac{7}{12}}$ 11. $3\frac{1}{9} + 2\frac{1}{3} = \mathbf{5\frac{4}{9}}$ 12. $5\frac{2}{3} + 7\frac{3}{7} = \mathbf{13\frac{2}{21}}$

13. $2\frac{5}{6} + 3\frac{1}{3} = \mathbf{6\frac{1}{6}}$ 14. $5\frac{1}{2} + 6\frac{2}{7} = \mathbf{11\frac{11}{14}}$ 15. $5\frac{5}{15} + 2\frac{3}{5} = \mathbf{7\frac{3}{5}}$

Page 37

Name _____ Date _____

Adding Mixed Numbers with Unlike Denominators

Total Problems:	15
Problems Correct:	_____

Solve each problem. Write each answer in simplest form.

1. $1\frac{1}{4}$ $+ 2\frac{5}{6}$ $\mathbf{4\frac{1}{12}}$
2. $6\frac{7}{12}$ $+ 8\frac{7}{13}$ $\mathbf{15\frac{19}{156}}$
3. $5\frac{10}{11}$ $+ 6\frac{3}{22}$ $\mathbf{12\frac{1}{22}}$
4. $10\frac{4}{5}$ $+ 7\frac{1}{8}$ $\mathbf{17\frac{37}{40}}$
5. $3\frac{3}{4}$ $+ 6\frac{1}{3}$ $\mathbf{10\frac{1}{12}}$

6. $9\frac{3}{5}$ $+ 6\frac{2}{3}$ $\mathbf{16\frac{4}{15}}$
7. $5\frac{1}{5}$ $+ 6\frac{2}{4}$ $\mathbf{11\frac{7}{10}}$
8. $3\frac{2}{3}$ $+ 4\frac{4}{5}$ $\mathbf{8\frac{7}{15}}$
9. $8\frac{1}{7}$ $+ 6\frac{2}{3}$ $\mathbf{14\frac{17}{21}}$
10. $2\frac{1}{5}$ $+ 6\frac{1}{4}$ $\mathbf{8\frac{9}{20}}$

11. $8\frac{5}{6}$ $+ 3\frac{3}{4}$ $\mathbf{12\frac{7}{12}}$
12. $5\frac{1}{3}$ $+ 2\frac{3}{4}$ $\mathbf{8\frac{1}{12}}$
13. $4\frac{1}{8}$ $+ 3\frac{1}{2}$ $\mathbf{7\frac{5}{8}}$
14. $8\frac{9}{10}$ $+ 4\frac{1}{4}$ $\mathbf{13\frac{3}{20}}$
15. $8\frac{1}{6}$ $+ 3\frac{3}{4}$ $\mathbf{11\frac{2}{3}}$

Page 38

Name _____ Date _____

Subtracting Fractions with Like Denominators

Total Problems:	20
Problems Correct:	_____

Solve each problem. Write each answer in simplest form.

1. $\frac{5}{6} - \frac{1}{6} = \mathbf{\frac{2}{3}}$ 2. $\frac{3}{4} - \frac{1}{4} = \mathbf{\frac{1}{2}}$ 3. $\frac{5}{9} - \frac{2}{9} = \mathbf{\frac{1}{3}}$ 4. $\frac{7}{8} - \frac{5}{8} = \mathbf{\frac{1}{4}}$

5. $\frac{3}{7} - \frac{2}{7} = \mathbf{\frac{1}{7}}$ 6. $\frac{7}{8} - \frac{3}{8} = \mathbf{\frac{1}{2}}$ 7. $\frac{5}{7} - \frac{2}{7} = \mathbf{\frac{3}{7}}$ 8. $\frac{5}{8} - \frac{1}{8} = \mathbf{\frac{1}{2}}$

9. $\frac{5}{9} - \frac{4}{9} = \mathbf{\frac{1}{9}}$ 10. $\frac{4}{6} - \frac{2}{6} = \mathbf{\frac{1}{3}}$ 11. $\frac{3}{10} - \frac{1}{10} = \mathbf{\frac{1}{5}}$ 12. $\frac{7}{9} - \frac{1}{9} = \mathbf{\frac{2}{3}}$

13. $\frac{3}{5} - \frac{2}{5} = \mathbf{\frac{1}{5}}$ 14. $\frac{5}{7} - \frac{3}{7} = \mathbf{\frac{2}{7}}$ 15. $\frac{2}{3} - \frac{1}{3} = \mathbf{\frac{1}{3}}$ 16. $\frac{15}{16} - \frac{7}{16} = \mathbf{\frac{1}{2}}$

17. $\frac{4}{5} - \frac{2}{5} = \mathbf{\frac{2}{5}}$ 18. $\frac{3}{6} - \frac{2}{6} = \mathbf{\frac{1}{6}}$ 19. $\frac{2}{5} - \frac{1}{5} = \mathbf{\frac{1}{5}}$ 20. $\frac{3}{4} - \frac{2}{4} = \mathbf{\frac{1}{4}}$

Page 39

Name _____ Date _____

Subtracting Fractions with Like Denominators

Total Problems:	20
Problems Correct:	_____

Solve each problem. Write each answer in simplest form.

1. $\frac{2}{5} - \frac{1}{5} = \mathbf{\frac{1}{5}}$ 2. $\frac{5}{7} - \frac{2}{7} = \mathbf{\frac{3}{7}}$ 3. $\frac{3}{5} - \frac{1}{5} = \mathbf{\frac{2}{5}}$ 4. $\frac{2}{8} - \frac{1}{8} = \mathbf{\frac{1}{8}}$

5. $\frac{2}{4} - \frac{1}{4} = \mathbf{\frac{1}{4}}$ 6. $\frac{7}{8} - \frac{3}{8} = \mathbf{\frac{1}{2}}$ 7. $\frac{2}{3} - \frac{1}{3} = \mathbf{\frac{1}{3}}$ 8. $\frac{7}{9} - \frac{5}{9} = \mathbf{\frac{2}{9}}$

9. $\frac{4}{6} - \frac{1}{6} = \mathbf{\frac{1}{2}}$ 10. $\frac{4}{7} - \frac{2}{7} = \mathbf{\frac{2}{7}}$ 11. $\frac{7}{10} - \frac{3}{10} = \mathbf{\frac{2}{5}}$ 12. $\frac{7}{8} - \frac{5}{8} = \mathbf{\frac{1}{4}}$

13. $\frac{3}{4} - \frac{2}{4} = \mathbf{\frac{1}{4}}$ 14. $\frac{5}{9} - \frac{1}{9} = \mathbf{\frac{4}{9}}$ 15. $\frac{4}{8} - \frac{1}{8} = \mathbf{\frac{3}{8}}$ 16. $\frac{11}{14} - \frac{9}{14} = \mathbf{\frac{1}{7}}$

17. $\frac{5}{6} - \frac{1}{6} = \mathbf{\frac{2}{3}}$ 18. $\frac{4}{5} - \frac{2}{5} = \mathbf{\frac{2}{5}}$ 19. $\frac{1}{2} - \frac{1}{2} = \mathbf{0}$ 20. $\frac{3}{5} - \frac{2}{5} = \mathbf{\frac{1}{5}}$

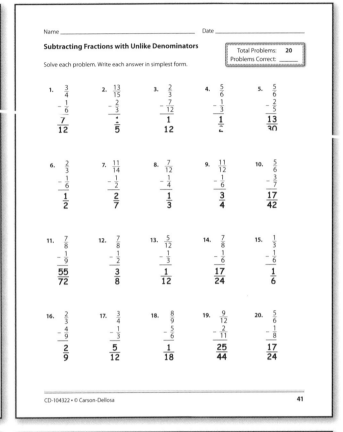

Worksheet (page 40)

Name _____ Date _____

Subtracting Fractions with Unlike Denominators

Total Problems: **20**
Problems Correct: _____

Solve each problem. Write each answer in simplest form.

1. $\frac{2}{9} - \frac{1}{4} = \frac{1}{12}$
2. $\frac{3}{4} - \frac{1}{5} = \frac{11}{20}$
3. $\frac{4}{5} - \frac{5}{10} = \frac{3}{10}$
4. $\frac{5}{7} - \frac{2}{9} = \frac{31}{63}$
5. $\frac{2}{3} - \frac{4}{9} = \frac{2}{9}$

6. $\frac{3}{8} - \frac{2}{6} = \frac{1}{24}$
7. $\frac{2}{4} - \frac{1}{3} = \frac{1}{6}$
8. $\frac{1}{5} - \frac{1}{8} = \frac{3}{40}$
9. $\frac{7}{12} - \frac{1}{4} = \frac{1}{3}$
10. $\frac{3}{9} - \frac{1}{3} = 0$

11. $\frac{7}{8} - \frac{1}{2} = \frac{3}{8}$
12. $\frac{8}{8} - \frac{4}{6} = \frac{1}{3}$
13. $\frac{2}{3} - \frac{1}{2} = \frac{1}{6}$
14. $\frac{1}{2} - \frac{1}{4} = \frac{1}{4}$
15. $\frac{1}{3} - \frac{1}{6} = \frac{1}{6}$

16. $\frac{8}{9} - \frac{3}{6} = \frac{7}{18}$
17. $\frac{5}{6} - \frac{1}{5} = \frac{19}{30}$
18. $\frac{7}{8} - \frac{3}{10} = \frac{23}{40}$
19. $\frac{9}{12} - \frac{2}{11} = \frac{25}{44}$
20. $\frac{6}{6} - \frac{3}{12} = \frac{3}{4}$

40 CD-104322 • © Carson-Dellosa

Worksheet (page 41)

Name _____ Date _____

Subtracting Fractions with Unlike Denominators

Total Problems: **20**
Problems Correct: _____

Solve each problem. Write each answer in simplest form.

1. $\frac{3}{4} - \frac{1}{6} = \frac{7}{12}$
2. $\frac{13}{15} - \frac{2}{3} = \frac{?}{5}$
3. $\frac{2}{3} - \frac{7}{12} = \frac{1}{12}$
4. $\frac{5}{6} - \frac{1}{3} = \frac{1}{2}$
5. $\frac{5}{6} - \frac{2}{5} = \frac{13}{30}$

6. $\frac{2}{3} - \frac{1}{6} = \frac{1}{2}$
7. $\frac{11}{14} - \frac{1}{2} = \frac{2}{7}$
8. $\frac{7}{12} - \frac{1}{4} = \frac{1}{3}$
9. $\frac{11}{12} - \frac{1}{6} = \frac{3}{4}$
10. $\frac{5}{6} - \frac{3}{7} = \frac{17}{42}$

11. $\frac{7}{8} - \frac{1}{9} = \frac{55}{72}$
12. $\frac{7}{8} - \frac{1}{2} = \frac{3}{8}$
13. $\frac{5}{12} - \frac{1}{3} = \frac{1}{12}$
14. $\frac{7}{8} - \frac{1}{6} = \frac{17}{24}$
15. $\frac{1}{3} - \frac{1}{6} = \frac{1}{6}$

16. $\frac{2}{3} - \frac{4}{9} = \frac{2}{9}$
17. $\frac{3}{4} - \frac{1}{3} = \frac{5}{12}$
18. $\frac{8}{9} - \frac{5}{6} = \frac{1}{18}$
19. $\frac{9}{12} - \frac{2}{11} = \frac{25}{44}$
20. $\frac{5}{6} - \frac{1}{8} = \frac{17}{24}$

CD-104322 • © Carson-Dellosa 41

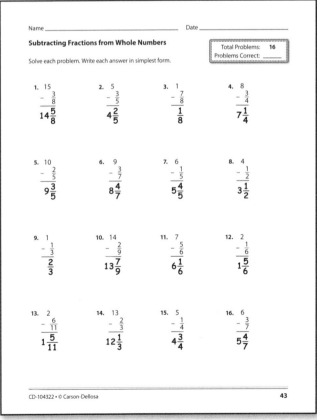

Worksheet (page 42)

Name _____ Date _____

Subtracting Fractions from Whole Numbers

Total Problems: **16**
Problems Correct: _____

Solve each problem. Write each answer in simplest form.

1. $2 - \frac{7}{8} = 1\frac{1}{8}$
2. $3 - \frac{3}{4} = 2\frac{1}{4}$
3. $5 - \frac{6}{9} = 4\frac{1}{3}$
4. $12 - \frac{5}{7} = 11\frac{2}{7}$

5. $4 - \frac{2}{5} = 3\frac{3}{5}$
6. $8 - \frac{9}{10} = 7\frac{1}{10}$
7. $4 - \frac{2}{6} = 3\frac{2}{3}$
8. $9 - \frac{1}{3} = 8\frac{2}{3}$

9. $5 - \frac{2}{3} = 4\frac{1}{3}$
10. $7 - \frac{4}{5} = 6\frac{1}{5}$
11. $5 - \frac{2}{5} = 4\frac{3}{5}$
12. $4 - \frac{7}{8} = 3\frac{1}{8}$

13. $6 - \frac{1}{8} = 5\frac{7}{8}$
14. $4 - \frac{3}{10} = 3\frac{7}{10}$
15. $10 - \frac{1}{2} = 9\frac{1}{2}$
16. $3 - \frac{6}{7} = 2\frac{1}{7}$

42 CD-104322 • © Carson-Dellosa

Worksheet (page 43)

Name _____ Date _____

Subtracting Fractions from Whole Numbers

Total Problems: **16**
Problems Correct: _____

Solve each problem. Write each answer in simplest form.

1. $15 - \frac{3}{8} = 14\frac{5}{8}$
2. $5 - \frac{3}{5} = 4\frac{2}{5}$
3. $1 - \frac{7}{8} = \frac{1}{8}$
4. $8 - \frac{3}{4} = 7\frac{1}{4}$

5. $10 - \frac{2}{5} = 9\frac{3}{5}$
6. $9 - \frac{3}{7} = 8\frac{4}{7}$
7. $6 - \frac{1}{5} = 5\frac{4}{5}$
8. $4 - \frac{1}{2} = 3\frac{1}{2}$

9. $1 - \frac{1}{3} = \frac{2}{3}$
10. $14 - \frac{2}{9} = 13\frac{7}{9}$
11. $7 - \frac{5}{6} = 6\frac{1}{6}$
12. $2 - \frac{1}{6} = 1\frac{5}{6}$

13. $2 - \frac{6}{11} = 1\frac{5}{11}$
14. $13 - \frac{2}{3} = 12\frac{1}{3}$
15. $5 - \frac{1}{4} = 4\frac{3}{4}$
16. $6 - \frac{3}{7} = 5\frac{4}{7}$

CD-104322 • © Carson-Dellosa 43

Subtracting Mixed Numbers with Like Denominators

Solve each problem. Write each answer in simplest form.

Total Problems: **16**
Problems Correct: _____

1. $8\frac{4}{5} - 1\frac{1}{5} = 7\frac{3}{5}$
2. $5\frac{3}{12} - 2\frac{17}{12} = 1\frac{5}{6}$
3. $5\frac{1}{3} - 4\frac{2}{3} = \frac{2}{3}$
4. $7\frac{3}{5} - 5\frac{1}{5} = 2\frac{2}{5}$

5. $5\frac{2}{3} - 4\frac{1}{3} = 1\frac{1}{3}$
6. $3\frac{3}{5} - 1\frac{4}{5} = 1\frac{4}{5}$
7. $5\frac{3}{8} - 3\frac{3}{8} = 2$
8. $4\frac{11}{13} - 2\frac{12}{13} = 1\frac{12}{13}$

9. $3\frac{1}{2} - 1\frac{1}{2} = 2$
10. $10\frac{9}{4} - 7\frac{1}{4} = 5$
11. $9\frac{6}{7} - 2\frac{2}{7} = 7\frac{4}{7}$
12. $7\frac{1}{6} - 5\frac{3}{6} = 1\frac{2}{3}$

13. $4\frac{2}{6} - 3\frac{5}{6} = \frac{1}{2}$
14. $6\frac{7}{8} - 1\frac{1}{8} = 5\frac{3}{4}$
15. $2\frac{1}{8} - 1\frac{1}{8} = 1$
16. $3\frac{7}{9} - 2\frac{1}{9} = 1\frac{2}{3}$

Subtracting Mixed Numbers with Unlike Denominators

Solve each problem. Write each answer in simplest form.

Total Problems: **16**
Problems Correct: _____

1. $12\frac{7}{8} - 5\frac{5}{16} = 7\frac{9}{16}$
2. $3\frac{1}{4} - 2\frac{5}{12} = \frac{5}{6}$
3. $10\frac{2}{3} - 9\frac{2}{9} = 1\frac{4}{9}$
4. $3\frac{1}{8} - 1\frac{7}{9} = 1\frac{25}{72}$

5. $10\frac{2}{5} - 7\frac{2}{3} = 2\frac{11}{15}$
6. $8\frac{7}{10} - 7\frac{9}{11} = \frac{97}{110}$
7. $8\frac{5}{10} - 7\frac{5}{12} = 1\frac{1}{12}$
8. $5\frac{12}{16} - 5\frac{11}{20} = \frac{1}{5}$

9. $6\frac{1}{6} - 5\frac{5}{12} = \frac{3}{4}$
10. $4\frac{5}{6} - 2\frac{1}{24} = 2\frac{19}{24}$
11. $8\frac{3}{16} - 7\frac{5}{32} = 1\frac{1}{32}$
12. $6\frac{1}{9} - 2\frac{1}{3} = 3\frac{7}{9}$

13. $2\frac{2}{3} - 1\frac{1}{5} = 1\frac{7}{15}$
14. $9\frac{3}{5} - 4\frac{9}{20} = 5\frac{3}{20}$
15. $4\frac{11}{18} - 1\frac{13}{16} = 2\frac{115}{144}$
16. $8\frac{7}{10} - 6\frac{3}{40} = 2\frac{5}{8}$

Multiplying Fractions

Solve each problem. Write each answer in simplest form.

Total Problems: **15**
Problems Correct: _____

1. $\frac{1}{4} \times \frac{2}{5} = \frac{1}{10}$
2. $\frac{2}{8} \times \frac{3}{6} = \frac{1}{8}$
3. $\frac{1}{6} \times \frac{4}{5} = \frac{2}{15}$

4. $\frac{1}{3} \times \frac{5}{6} = \frac{5}{18}$
5. $\frac{4}{6} \times \frac{5}{7} = \frac{10}{21}$
6. $\frac{3}{5} \times \frac{1}{8} = \frac{3}{40}$

7. $\frac{5}{7} \times \frac{2}{4} = \frac{5}{14}$
8. $\frac{3}{4} \times \frac{4}{7} = \frac{3}{7}$
9. $\frac{3}{4} \times \frac{5}{5} = \frac{3}{4}$

10. $\frac{1}{6} \times \frac{4}{5} = \frac{2}{15}$
11. $\frac{5}{6} \times \frac{3}{4} = \frac{5}{8}$
12. $\frac{3}{5} \times \frac{3}{7} = \frac{9}{35}$

13. $\frac{2}{5} \times \frac{4}{9} = \frac{8}{45}$
14. $\frac{2}{8} \times \frac{3}{3} = \frac{1}{4}$
15. $\frac{1}{7} \times \frac{3}{4} = \frac{3}{28}$

Multiplying Fractions

Solve each problem. Write each answer in simplest form.

Total Problems: **15**
Problems Correct: _____

1. $\frac{5}{8} \times \frac{3}{4} = \frac{15}{32}$
2. $\frac{3}{4} \times \frac{2}{7} = \frac{3}{14}$
3. $\frac{5}{7} \times \frac{3}{7} = \frac{15}{49}$

4. $\frac{1}{2} \times \frac{3}{5} = \frac{3}{10}$
5. $\frac{3}{6} \times \frac{7}{8} = \frac{7}{16}$
6. $\frac{2}{9} \times \frac{4}{6} = \frac{4}{27}$

7. $\frac{1}{2} \times \frac{5}{9} = \frac{5}{18}$
8. $\frac{3}{8} \times \frac{1}{4} = \frac{3}{32}$
9. $\frac{1}{4} \times \frac{3}{7} = \frac{3}{28}$

10. $\frac{4}{5} \times \frac{5}{6} = \frac{2}{3}$
11. $\frac{1}{2} \times \frac{3}{7} = \frac{3}{14}$
12. $\frac{2}{3} \times \frac{3}{5} = \frac{2}{5}$

13. $\frac{2}{6} \times \frac{2}{5} = \frac{2}{15}$
14. $\frac{8}{9} \times \frac{1}{6} = \frac{4}{27}$
15. $\frac{3}{6} \times \frac{8}{9} = \frac{12}{27}$

Worksheet (page 48) — Multiplying Fractions

Name _____ Date _____

Multiplying Fractions

Total Problems: 15
Problems Correct: _____

Solve each problem. Write each answer in simplest form.

1. $\frac{3}{4} \times \frac{2}{5} = \frac{3}{10}$ 2. $\frac{7}{8} \times \frac{1}{2} = \frac{7}{16}$ 3. $\frac{4}{5} \times \frac{2}{3} = \frac{8}{15}$

4. $\frac{1}{3} \times \frac{1}{5} = \frac{1}{15}$ 5. $\frac{2}{7} \times \frac{2}{9} = \frac{4}{63}$ 6. $\frac{1}{4} \times \frac{3}{5} = \frac{3}{20}$

7. $\frac{4}{7} \times \frac{3}{8} = \frac{3}{14}$ 8. $\frac{2}{3} \times \frac{2}{5} = \frac{4}{15}$ 9. $\frac{1}{3} \times \frac{4}{5} = \frac{4}{15}$

10. $\frac{3}{5} \times \frac{1}{3} = \frac{1}{5}$ 11. $\frac{1}{8} \times \frac{2}{5} = \frac{1}{20}$ 12. $\frac{1}{6} \times \frac{2}{3} = \frac{1}{9}$

13. $\frac{1}{2} \times \frac{3}{4} = \frac{3}{8}$ 14. $\frac{1}{8} \times \frac{1}{3} = \frac{1}{24}$ 15. $\frac{2}{8} \times \frac{3}{4} = \frac{3}{16}$

Worksheet (page 49) — Multiplying Fractions

Name _____ Date _____

Multiplying Fractions

Total Problems: 15
Problems Correct: _____

Solve each problem. Write each answer in simplest form.

1. $\frac{1}{3} \times \frac{1}{7} = \frac{1}{21}$ 2. $\frac{3}{5} \times \frac{2}{9} = \frac{2}{15}$ 3. $\frac{1}{6} \times \frac{4}{5} = \frac{2}{15}$

4. $\frac{2}{7} \times \frac{5}{8} = \frac{5}{28}$ 5. $\frac{2}{5} \times \frac{4}{9} = \frac{8}{45}$ 6. $\frac{1}{4} \times \frac{1}{6} = \frac{1}{24}$

7. $\frac{2}{3} \times \frac{3}{8} = \frac{1}{4}$ 8. $\frac{3}{4} \times \frac{4}{7} = \frac{3}{7}$ 9. $\frac{2}{5} \times \frac{5}{6} = \frac{1}{3}$

10. $\frac{4}{5} \times \frac{2}{3} = \frac{8}{15}$ 11. $\frac{1}{5} \times \frac{5}{6} = \frac{1}{6}$ 12. $\frac{1}{2} \times \frac{3}{7} = \frac{3}{14}$

13. $\frac{2}{5} \times \frac{5}{9} = \frac{2}{9}$ 14. $\frac{2}{8} \times \frac{3}{3} = \frac{1}{4}$ 15. $\frac{5}{6} \times \frac{2}{7} = \frac{5}{21}$

Worksheet (page 50) — Multiplying Fractions and Whole Numbers

Name _____ Date _____

Multiplying Fractions and Whole Numbers

Total Problems: 15
Problems Correct: _____

Solve each problem. Write each answer in simplest form.

1. $4 \times \frac{1}{2} = 2$ 2. $2 \times \frac{2}{5} = \frac{4}{5}$ 3. $4 \times \frac{2}{7} = 1\frac{1}{7}$

4. $3 \times \frac{5}{6} = 2\frac{1}{2}$ 5. $8 \times \frac{1}{8} = 1$ 6. $\frac{2}{5} \times 3 = 1\frac{1}{5}$

7. $\frac{1}{8} \times 5 = \frac{5}{8}$ 8. $\frac{5}{7} \times 5 = 3\frac{4}{7}$ 9. $\frac{2}{3} \times 2 = 1\frac{1}{3}$

10. $\frac{3}{9} \times 4 = 1\frac{1}{3}$ 11. $\frac{1}{3} \times 7 = 2\frac{1}{3}$ 12. $4 \times \frac{3}{4} = 3$

13. $\frac{6}{8} \times 2 = 1\frac{1}{2}$ 14. $5 \times \frac{4}{5} = 4$ 15. $8 \times \frac{2}{5} = 3\frac{1}{5}$

Worksheet (page 51) — Multiplying Fractions and Whole Numbers

Name _____ Date _____

Multiplying Fractions and Whole Numbers

Total Problems: 15
Problems Correct: _____

Solve each problem. Write each answer in simplest form.

1. $5 \times \frac{2}{5} = 2$ 2. $8 \times \frac{1}{7} = 1\frac{1}{7}$ 3. $6 \times \frac{3}{8} = 2\frac{1}{4}$

4. $4 \times \frac{8}{9} = 3\frac{5}{9}$ 5. $2 \times \frac{3}{7} = \frac{6}{7}$ 6. $\frac{2}{3} \times 4 = 2\frac{2}{3}$

7. $\frac{1}{9} \times 6 = \frac{2}{3}$ 8. $\frac{5}{6} \times 4 = 3\frac{1}{3}$ 9. $\frac{4}{6} \times 3 = 2$

10. $\frac{4}{5} \times 6 = 4\frac{4}{5}$ 11. $\frac{3}{4} \times 5 = 3\frac{3}{4}$ 12. $2 \times \frac{4}{5} = 1\frac{3}{5}$

13. $\frac{2}{7} \times 6 = 1\frac{5}{7}$ 14. $7 \times \frac{3}{5} = 4\frac{1}{5}$ 15. $9 \times \frac{3}{4} = 6\frac{3}{4}$

Name _____ **Date** _____

Multiplying Fractions and Whole Numbers

Total Problems: 15
Problems Correct: _____

Solve each problem. Write each answer in simplest form.

1. $10 \times \frac{2}{3} =$ **$6\frac{2}{3}$**   2. $4 \times \frac{4}{7} =$ **$2\frac{2}{7}$**   3. $7 \times \frac{10}{11} =$ **$6\frac{4}{11}$**

4. $36 \times \frac{2}{288} =$ **$\frac{1}{4}$**   5. $6 \times \frac{4}{8} =$ **3**   6. $9 \times \frac{5}{6} =$ **$7\frac{1}{2}$**

7. $3 \times \frac{1}{3} =$ **1**   8. $30 \times \frac{3}{90} =$ **1**   9. $12 \times \frac{1}{36} =$ **$\frac{1}{3}$**

10. $5 \times \frac{2}{5} =$ **2**   11. $12 \times \frac{7}{8} =$ **$10\frac{1}{2}$**   12. $5 \times \frac{3}{4} =$ **$3\frac{3}{4}$**

13. $22 \times \frac{1}{44} =$ **$\frac{1}{2}$**   14. $4 \times \frac{1}{8} =$ **$\frac{1}{2}$**   15. $11 \times \frac{3}{8} =$ **$4\frac{1}{8}$**

Name _____ **Date** _____

Multiplying Mixed Numbers and Whole Numbers

Total Problems: 12
Problems Correct: _____

Solve each problem. Write each answer in simplest form.

1. $2 \times 2\frac{1}{3} =$ **$4\frac{2}{3}$**   2. $3 \times 5\frac{1}{5} =$ **$15\frac{3}{5}$**   3. $9 \times 3\frac{2}{3} =$ **33**

4. $8 \times 9\frac{1}{10} =$ **$72\frac{4}{5}$**   5. $4 \times 5\frac{1}{8} =$ **$20\frac{1}{2}$**   6. $6 \times 3\frac{1}{6} =$ **19**

7. $5 \times 6\frac{5}{8} =$ **$33\frac{1}{8}$**   8. $3 \times 9\frac{1}{3} =$ **28**   9. $7 \times 1\frac{3}{4} =$ **$12\frac{1}{4}$**

10. $7 \times 2\frac{3}{5} =$ **$18\frac{1}{5}$**   11. $4 \times 2\frac{1}{2} =$ **10**   12. $7 \times 2\frac{1}{7} =$ **15**

Name _____ **Date** _____

Multiplying Mixed Numbers and Whole Numbers

Total Problems: 12
Problems Correct: _____

Solve each problem. Write each answer in simplest form.

1. $4 \times 3\frac{3}{5} =$ **$14\frac{2}{5}$**   2. $6 \times 9\frac{4}{5} =$ **$58\frac{4}{5}$**   3. $2 \times 8\frac{3}{4} =$ **$17\frac{1}{2}$**

4. $9 \times 1\frac{1}{18} =$ **$9\frac{1}{2}$**   5. $10 \times 5\frac{1}{2} =$ **55**   6. $8 \times 2\frac{3}{8} =$ **19**

7. $5 \times 4\frac{2}{5} =$ **22**   8. $2 \times 7\frac{5}{8} =$ **$15\frac{1}{4}$**   9. $2 \times 5\frac{1}{8} =$ **$10\frac{1}{4}$**

10. $3 \times 1\frac{15}{16} =$ **$5\frac{13}{16}$**   11. $4 \times 8\frac{6}{7} =$ **$35\frac{3}{7}$**   12. $2 \times 2\frac{1}{4} =$ **$4\frac{1}{2}$**

Name _____ **Date** _____

Multiplying Mixed Numbers

Total Problems: 12
Problems Correct: _____

Solve each problem. Write each answer in simplest form.

1. $3\frac{1}{2} \times 2\frac{1}{2} =$ **$8\frac{3}{4}$**   2. $8\frac{5}{6} \times 3\frac{6}{7} =$ **$34\frac{1}{14}$**   3. $4\frac{2}{5} \times 6\frac{2}{3} =$ **$29\frac{1}{3}$**

4. $4\frac{2}{9} \times 5\frac{10}{11} =$ **$24\frac{94}{99}$**   5. $2\frac{2}{3} \times 4\frac{2}{5} =$ **$11\frac{11}{15}$**   6. $5\frac{3}{4} \times 6\frac{1}{4} =$ **$35\frac{15}{16}$**

7. $2\frac{8}{9} \times 7\frac{7}{8} =$ **$22\frac{3}{4}$**   8. $7\frac{1}{4} \times 3\frac{3}{7} =$ **$24\frac{6}{7}$**   9. $6\frac{7}{8} \times 3\frac{1}{3} =$ **$22\frac{11}{12}$**

10. $7\frac{9}{10} \times 8\frac{7}{8} =$ **$70\frac{9}{80}$**   11. $4\frac{1}{4} \times 3\frac{5}{6} =$ **$16\frac{7}{24}$**   12. $8\frac{3}{5} \times 1\frac{1}{2} =$ **$12\frac{9}{10}$**

Name _____ Date _____

Multiplying Mixed Numbers

Total Problems: **12**
Problems Correct: _____

Solve each problem. Write each answer in simplest form.

1. $8\frac{1}{4} \times 6\frac{2}{3} = $ **55**   2. $7\frac{2}{5} \times 9\frac{1}{8} = 67\frac{21}{40}$ 3. $2\frac{5}{6} \times 12\frac{4}{5} = 36\frac{4}{15}$

4. $4\frac{2}{7} \times 6\frac{1}{10} = 26\frac{1}{7}$ 5. $2\frac{9}{10} \times 5\frac{7}{8} = 17\frac{3}{80}$ 6. $5\frac{1}{3} \times 4\frac{1}{2} = $ **24**

7. $3\frac{1}{3} \times 3\frac{1}{3} = 11\frac{1}{9}$ 8. $3\frac{3}{4} \times 2\frac{1}{3} = 8\frac{3}{4}$ 9. $5\frac{1}{5} \times 4\frac{1}{3} = 22\frac{8}{15}$

10. $9\frac{9}{10} \times 4\frac{7}{8} = 48\frac{21}{80}$ 11. $1\frac{10}{13} \times 2\frac{9}{13} = 4\frac{129}{169}$ 12. $8\frac{3}{5} \times 4\frac{5}{6} = 41\frac{17}{30}$

56   CD-104322 • © Carson-Dellosa

Name _____ Date _____

Finding the Reciprocal

Total Problems: **16**
Problems Correct: _____

Find the reciprocal of each fraction or whole number.

1. $\frac{3}{5}$ $\frac{5}{3}$ 2. $\frac{2}{3}$ $\frac{3}{2}$ 3. 9 $\frac{1}{9}$ 4. $\frac{5}{3}$ $\frac{3}{5}$

5. $\frac{7}{3}$ $\frac{3}{7}$ 6. $\frac{6}{3}$ $\frac{3}{6}$ 7. $\frac{1}{12}$ 12 8. $\frac{9}{10}$ $\frac{10}{9}$

9. $\frac{2}{17}$ $\frac{17}{2}$ 10. $\frac{9}{1}$ $\frac{1}{9}$ 11. 6 $\frac{1}{6}$ 12. $\frac{4}{2}$ $\frac{2}{4}$

Change each mixed number to an improper fraction. Then, find its reciprocal.

	Fraction	Reciprocal
13. $2\frac{3}{5} = $	$\frac{13}{5}$	$\frac{5}{13}$
14. $1\frac{3}{4} = $	$\frac{7}{4}$	$\frac{4}{7}$
15. $3\frac{7}{8} = $	$\frac{31}{8}$	$\frac{8}{31}$
16. $6\frac{2}{5} = $	$\frac{32}{5}$	$\frac{5}{32}$

CD-104322 • © Carson-Dellosa   57

Name _____ Date _____

Dividing Fractions

Total Problems: **15**
Problems Correct: _____

Solve each problem. Write each answer in simplest form.

1. $\frac{3}{5} \div \frac{5}{6} = \frac{18}{25}$ 2. $\frac{5}{8} \div \frac{3}{5} = 1\frac{1}{24}$ 3. $\frac{7}{10} \div \frac{3}{5} = 1\frac{1}{6}$

4. $\frac{4}{7} \div \frac{3}{7} = 1\frac{1}{3}$ 5. $\frac{3}{5} \div \frac{7}{8} = \frac{24}{35}$ 6. $\frac{3}{16} \div \frac{3}{8} = \frac{1}{2}$

7. $\frac{4}{9} \div \frac{3}{4} = \frac{16}{27}$ 8. $\frac{7}{8} \div \frac{2}{3} = 1\frac{5}{16}$ 9. $\frac{1}{6} \div \frac{4}{5} = \frac{5}{24}$

10. $\frac{3}{4} \div \frac{3}{5} = 1\frac{1}{4}$ 11. $\frac{7}{9} \div \frac{2}{3} = 1\frac{1}{6}$ 12. $\frac{7}{8} \div \frac{5}{11} = 1\frac{37}{40}$

13. $\frac{2}{5} \div \frac{3}{8} = 1\frac{1}{15}$ 14. $\frac{2}{3} \div \frac{4}{5} = \frac{5}{6}$ 15. $\frac{5}{9} \div \frac{2}{8} = 2\frac{2}{9}$

58   CD-104322 • © Carson-Dellosa

Name _____ Date _____

Dividing Fractions and Whole Numbers

Total Problems: **15**
Problems Correct: _____

Solve each problem. Write each answer in simplest form.

1. $8 \div \frac{6}{7} = 9\frac{1}{3}$ 2. $3 \div \frac{1}{2} = $ **6**   3. $12 \div \frac{3}{4} = $ **16**

4. $14 \div \frac{7}{8} = $ **16**   5. $5 \div \frac{1}{3} = $ **15**   6. $\frac{5}{6} \div 10 = \frac{1}{12}$

7. $\frac{2}{3} \div 6 = \frac{1}{9}$ 8. $\frac{3}{4} \div 4 = \frac{3}{16}$ 9. $\frac{1}{2} \div 6 = \frac{1}{12}$

10. $\frac{1}{4} \div 2 = \frac{1}{8}$ 11. $\frac{2}{5} \div 3 = \frac{2}{15}$ 12. $10 \div \frac{6}{7} = 11\frac{2}{3}$

13. $\frac{4}{7} \div 5 = \frac{4}{35}$ 14. $6 \div \frac{1}{5} = $ **30**   15. $12 \div \frac{3}{9} = $ **36**

CD-104322 • © Carson-Dellosa   59

Page 60

Name _____ Date _____

Dividing Fractions and Mixed Numbers

Solve each problem. Write each answer in simplest form.

Total Problems: **12**
Problems Correct: _____

1. $1\frac{1}{6} \div \frac{1}{4} =$ **$4\frac{2}{3}$**
2. $3\frac{1}{4} \div \frac{3}{8} =$ **$8\frac{2}{3}$**
3. $5\frac{2}{3} \div \frac{9}{10} =$ **$6\frac{8}{27}$**

4. $1\frac{4}{5} \div \frac{2}{7} =$ **$6\frac{3}{10}$**
5. $2\frac{3}{4} \div \frac{1}{8} =$ **22**
6. $2\frac{1}{2} \div \frac{1}{2} =$ **5**

7. $2\frac{1}{4} \div \frac{3}{8} =$ **6**
8. $4\frac{1}{2} \div \frac{1}{2} =$ **9**
9. $6\frac{1}{8} \div \frac{4}{7} =$ **$10\frac{23}{32}$**

10. $2\frac{3}{4} \div \frac{1}{2} =$ **$5\frac{1}{2}$**
11. $1\frac{1}{4} \div \frac{2}{3} =$ **$1\frac{7}{8}$**
12. $1\frac{2}{5} \div \frac{1}{3} =$ **$4\frac{1}{5}$**

60
CD-104322 • © Carson-Dellosa

Page 61

Name _____ Date _____

Dividing Fractions and Mixed Numbers

Solve each problem. Write each answer in simplest form.

Total Problems: **12**
Problems Correct: _____

1. $1\frac{1}{6} \div \frac{1}{4} =$ **$4\frac{2}{3}$**
2. $2\frac{2}{5} \div \frac{2}{3} =$ **$3\frac{3}{5}$**
3. $6\frac{3}{8} \div \frac{7}{10} =$ **$9\frac{3}{28}$**

4. $1\frac{1}{3} \div \frac{7}{8} =$ **$1\frac{11}{21}$**
5. $3\frac{1}{2} \div \frac{1}{4} =$ **14**
6. $5\frac{1}{3} \div \frac{3}{8} =$ **$14\frac{2}{9}$**

7. $3\frac{1}{3} \div \frac{3}{4} =$ **$4\frac{4}{9}$**
8. $2\frac{1}{3} \div 5 =$ **$\frac{7}{15}$**
9. $1\frac{1}{3} \div \frac{8}{3} =$ **$\frac{1}{2}$**

10. $3\frac{3}{5} \div 10 =$ **$\frac{9}{25}$**
11. $1\frac{1}{5} \div \frac{2}{5} =$ **3**
12. $5\frac{6}{7} \div \frac{3}{4} =$ **$7\frac{17}{21}$**

CD-104322 • © Carson-Dellosa
61

Page 62

Name _____ Date _____

Dividing Mixed Numbers

Solve each problem. Write each answer in simplest form.

Total Problems: **12**
Problems Correct: _____

1. $2\frac{1}{3} \div 4\frac{1}{5} =$ **$\frac{5}{9}$**
2. $5\frac{1}{2} \div 1\frac{1}{8} =$ **$4\frac{8}{9}$**
3. $3\frac{1}{3} \div 1\frac{1}{9} =$ **3**

4. $2\frac{2}{3} \div 2\frac{2}{5} =$ **$1\frac{1}{9}$**
5. $5\frac{1}{4} \div 2\frac{1}{3} =$ **$2\frac{1}{4}$**
6. $7\frac{3}{8} \div 1\frac{5}{8} =$ **$4\frac{7}{13}$**

7. $5\frac{2}{3} \div 1\frac{6}{7} =$ **$3\frac{2}{39}$**
8. $2\frac{2}{5} \div 3\frac{7}{10} =$ **$\frac{24}{37}$**
9. $6\frac{1}{3} \div 3\frac{5}{6} =$ **$1\frac{15}{23}$**

10. $6\frac{3}{8} \div 2\frac{5}{6} =$ **$2\frac{1}{4}$**
11. $7\frac{1}{9} \div 5\frac{1}{3} =$ **$1\frac{1}{3}$**
12. $7\frac{2}{5} \div 5\frac{2}{3} =$ **$1\frac{26}{85}$**

62
CD-104322 • © Carson-Dellosa

Page 63

Name _____ Date _____

Dividing Mixed Numbers

Solve each problem. Write each answer in simplest form.

Total Problems: **12**
Problems Correct: _____

1. $8\frac{3}{4} \div 5\frac{2}{5} =$ **$1\frac{67}{108}$**
2. $9\frac{3}{5} \div 8\frac{2}{3} =$ **$1\frac{7}{65}$**
3. $3\frac{1}{3} \div 5\frac{3}{5} =$ **$\frac{25}{42}$**

4. $1\frac{3}{7} \div 2\frac{2}{3} =$ **$\frac{15}{28}$**
5. $1\frac{3}{5} \div 2\frac{1}{2} =$ **$\frac{16}{25}$**
6. $2\frac{1}{5} \div 1\frac{3}{4} =$ **$1\frac{9}{35}$**

7. $2\frac{1}{2} \div 3\frac{8}{9} =$ **$\frac{9}{14}$**
8. $4\frac{2}{3} \div 5\frac{9}{10} =$ **$\frac{140}{177}$**
9. $3\frac{3}{5} \div 3\frac{3}{4} =$ **$\frac{24}{25}$**

10. $5\frac{2}{5} \div 6\frac{5}{8} =$ **$\frac{216}{265}$**
11. $6\frac{3}{4} \div 2\frac{5}{8} =$ **$2\frac{4}{7}$**
12. $4\frac{3}{8} \div 3\frac{3}{5} =$ **$1\frac{31}{144}$**

CD-104322 • © Carson-Dellosa
63

Worksheet 1 (page 64)

Name _____ Date _____

Multiplying and Dividing Fractions Review

Solve each problem. Write each answer in simplest form.

Total Problems: 12
Problems Correct: _____

1. $1\frac{1}{5} \div 2\frac{1}{4} = \frac{8}{15}$ 2. $6\frac{7}{8} \div 1\frac{1}{3} = 5\frac{5}{32}$ 3. $3\frac{1}{5} \times 2\frac{1}{10} = 6\frac{18}{25}$

4. $1\frac{4}{5} \times 3\frac{5}{5} = 7\frac{1}{5}$ 5. $1\frac{4}{5} \div 1\frac{1}{5} = 1\frac{1}{2}$ 6. $2\frac{1}{2} \div 1\frac{1}{2} = 1\frac{2}{3}$

7. $2\frac{1}{3} \times 3\frac{1}{3} = 7\frac{7}{9}$ 8. $4\frac{2}{6} \times 3\frac{7}{18} = 14\frac{37}{54}$ 9. $2\frac{3}{5} \times 1\frac{1}{2} = 3\frac{9}{10}$

10. $4\frac{1}{2} \div 1\frac{1}{5} = 3\frac{3}{4}$ 11. $3\frac{3}{4} \times 2\frac{2}{6} = 8\frac{3}{4}$ 12. $3\frac{3}{8} \div 3\frac{3}{8} = 1$

Worksheet 2 (page 65)

Name _____ Date _____

Multiplying and Dividing Fractions Review

Solve each problem. Write each answer in simplest form.

Total Problems: 12
Problems Correct: _____

1. $3\frac{1}{3} \div 1\frac{1}{2} = 2\frac{2}{9}$ 2. $5\frac{1}{2} \div 1\frac{1}{4} = 4\frac{2}{5}$ 3. $2\frac{1}{6} \times 1\frac{1}{12} = 2\frac{25}{72}$

4. $2\frac{3}{6} \times 4\frac{5}{10} = 11\frac{1}{4}$ 5. $2\frac{3}{5} \div 2\frac{3}{5} = 1\frac{2}{11}$ 6. $2\frac{1}{4} \times 1\frac{1}{4} = 2\frac{13}{16}$

7. $3\frac{2}{4} \div 1\frac{3}{5} = 2\frac{11}{12}$ 8. $2\frac{2}{8} \times 4\frac{5}{16} = 9\frac{45}{64}$ 9. $3\frac{1}{2} \times 3\frac{1}{2} = 12\frac{1}{4}$

10. $4\frac{1}{6} \div 1\frac{1}{6} = 3\frac{4}{7}$ 11. $2\frac{3}{5} \div 1\frac{3}{5} = 1\frac{6}{7}$ 12. $3\frac{3}{5} \times 3\frac{3}{5} = 12\frac{24}{25}$

Worksheet 3 (page 66)

Name _____ Date _____

Understanding Decimals

Complete the chart. Fill in the whole number, tenths, hundredths, and thousandths columns with the correct number. Use zeros as placeholders where necessary.

Total Problems: 11
Problems Correct: _____

	Number	Whole Number	Tenths	Hundredths	Thousandths
1.	3.751	3	7	5	1
2.	4.891	4	8	9	1
3.	1.608	1	6	0	8
4.	10.540	10	5	4	0
5.	9.618	9	6	1	8
6.	2.198	2	1	9	8
7.	0.208	0	2	0	8
8.	0.005	0	0	0	5
9.	1.7	1	7		
10.	2.398	2	3	9	8
11.	6.0	6	0		

Worksheet 4 (page 67)

Name _____ Date _____

Understanding Decimals

Total Problems: 16
Problems Correct: _____

Write a decimal for each of the following descriptions.

1. One tenth __0.1__

2. Twenty-seven hundredths __0.27__

3. Three thousandths __0.003__

4. Seven tenths __0.7__

5. Forty-five hundredths __0.45__

6. Fifty-one thousandths __0.051__

Write each decimal in words.

7. 0.047 __Forty-seven thousandths__

8. 0.99 __Ninety-nine hundredths__

9. 0.8 __Eight tenths__

10. 0.809 __Eight hundred nine thousandths__

11. 0.06 __Six hundredths__

Order the numbers in each series from smallest to largest.

12. 1.871, 0.1871, 10.871 __0.1871, 1.871, 10.871__

13. 0.045, 0.45, 0.04 __0.04, 0.045, 0.45__

14. 0.0065, 0.06, 0.006 __0.006, 0.0065, 0.06__

15. 0.91, 0.44, 0.23 __0.23, 0.44, 0.91__

16. 6.07, 6.17, 6.37 __6.07, 6.17, 6.37__

Name _____ Date _____

Writing Decimals as Fractions

	Total Problems:	16
	Problems Correct:	_____

Write each decimal as a fraction. Write the answer in simplest form.

1. $0.25 = \dfrac{1}{4}$ 2. $0.15 = \dfrac{3}{20}$ 3. $0.035 = \dfrac{7}{200}$ 4. $0.17 = \dfrac{17}{100}$

5. $0.75 = \dfrac{3}{4}$ 6. $0.30 = \dfrac{3}{10}$ 7. $0.125 = \dfrac{1}{8}$ 8. $0.50 = \dfrac{1}{2}$

9. $0.033 = \dfrac{33}{1000}$ 10. $0.075 = \dfrac{3}{40}$ 11. $0.60 = \dfrac{3}{5}$ 12. $0.018 = \dfrac{9}{500}$

13. $0.6 = \dfrac{3}{5}$ 14. $0.025 = \dfrac{1}{40}$ 15. $0.185 = \dfrac{37}{200}$ 16. $0.611 = \dfrac{611}{1000}$

Name _____ Date _____

Writing Decimals as Fractions

	Total Problems:	16
	Problems Correct:	_____

Write each decimal as a fraction. Write the answer in simplest form.

1. $0.625 = \dfrac{5}{8}$ 2. $0.008 = \dfrac{1}{125}$ 3. $0.60 = \dfrac{3}{5}$ 4. $0.23 = \dfrac{23}{100}$

5. $0.020 = \dfrac{1}{50}$ 6. $0.054 = \dfrac{27}{500}$ 7. $0.075 = \dfrac{3}{40}$ 8. $0.001 = \dfrac{1}{1000}$

9. $0.100 = \dfrac{1}{10}$ 10. $0.012 = \dfrac{3}{250}$ 11. $0.033 = \dfrac{33}{1000}$ 12. $0.12 = \dfrac{3}{25}$

13. $0.03 = \dfrac{3}{100}$ 14. $0.219 = \dfrac{219}{1000}$ 15. $0.575 = \dfrac{23}{40}$ 16. $0.35 = \dfrac{7}{20}$

Name _____ Date _____

Writing Decimals as Fractions

	Total Problems:	16
	Problems Correct:	_____

Write each decimal as a fraction. Write the answer in simplest form.

1. $0.5 = \dfrac{1}{2}$ 2. $0.05 = \dfrac{1}{20}$ 3. $0.075 = \dfrac{3}{40}$ 4. $0.12 = \dfrac{3}{25}$

5. $0.333 = \dfrac{333}{1000}$ 6. $0.25 = \dfrac{1}{4}$ 7. $0.15 = \dfrac{3}{20}$ 8. $0.54 = \dfrac{27}{50}$

9. $0.1 = \dfrac{1}{10}$ 10. $0.08 = \dfrac{2}{25}$ 11. $0.125 = \dfrac{1}{8}$ 12. $0.2 = \dfrac{1}{5}$

13. $0.8 = \dfrac{4}{5}$ 14. $0.143 = \dfrac{143}{1000}$ 15. $0.625 = \dfrac{5}{8}$ 16. $0.025 = \dfrac{1}{40}$

Name _____ Date _____

Writing Decimals as Fractions

	Total Problems:	16
	Problems Correct:	_____

Write each decimal as a fraction or mixed number. Write the answer in simplest form.

1. $0.009 = \dfrac{9}{1000}$ 2. $0.41 = \dfrac{41}{100}$ 3. $3.5 = 3\dfrac{1}{2}$ 4. $4.014 = 4\dfrac{7}{500}$

5. $0.019 = \dfrac{19}{1000}$ 6. $0.15 = \dfrac{3}{20}$ 7. $4.03 = 4\dfrac{3}{100}$ 8. $0.5 = \dfrac{1}{2}$

9. $0.933 = \dfrac{933}{1000}$ 10. $0.183 = \dfrac{183}{1000}$ 11. $2.62 = 2\dfrac{31}{50}$ 12. $0.09 = \dfrac{9}{100}$

13. $0.3 = \dfrac{3}{10}$ 14. $0.025 = \dfrac{1}{40}$ 15. $3.25 = 3\dfrac{1}{4}$ 16. $6.17 = 6\dfrac{17}{100}$

Page 72

Name _____   Date _____

Writing Fractions as Decimals

Total Problems: 12
Problems Correct: _____

Write each fraction or mixed number as a decimal.

1. $\frac{6}{10}$ = **0.6**   2. $\frac{3}{10}$ = **0.3**   3. $3\frac{8}{10}$ = **3.8**

4. $4\frac{15}{1,000}$ = **4.015**   5. $\frac{7}{100}$ = **0.07**   6. $\frac{4}{100}$ = **0.04**

7. $2\frac{9}{10}$ = **2.9**   8. $\frac{8}{1,000}$ = **0.008**   9. $\frac{27}{100}$ = **0.27**

10. $\frac{50}{100}$ = **0.50**   11. $\frac{142}{1,000}$ = **0.142**   12. $\frac{7}{100}$ = **0.07**

72   CD-104322 • © Carson-Dellosa

Page 73

Name _____   Date _____

Writing Fractions as Decimals

Total Problems: 16
Problems Correct: _____

Write each fraction or mixed number as a decimal. Round to the nearest thousandth when necessary.

1. $5\frac{7}{8}$ = **5.875**   2. $\frac{47}{50}$ = **0.94**   3. $\frac{1}{2}$ = **0.5**   4. $\frac{9}{200}$ = **0.045**

5. $3\frac{4}{5}$ = **3.8**   6. $\frac{3}{8}$ = **0.375**   7. $\frac{1}{5}$ = **0.2**   8. $\frac{7}{25}$ = **0.28**

9. $4\frac{3}{5}$ = **4.6**   10. $\frac{3}{4}$ = **0.75**   11. $\frac{1}{4}$ = **0.25**   12. $\frac{7}{20}$ = **0.35**

13. $2\frac{1}{5}$ = **2.2**   14. $\frac{1}{8}$ = **0.125**   15. $\frac{1}{3}$ = **0.333**   16. $\frac{4}{5}$ = **0.8**

CD-104322 • © Carson-Dellosa   73

Page 74

Name _____   Date _____

Adding Decimals

Total Problems: 20
Problems Correct: _____

Solve each problem.

1. 2.4 + 1.7 = **4.1**
2. 18.6 + 9.5 = **28.1**
3. 0.01 + 0.72 = **0.73**
4. 3.2 + 1.4 + 7.8 = **12.4**
5. 2.016 + 3.094 + 8.627 = **13.737**

6. 8.1 + 9.2 = **17.3**
7. 14.3 + 1.9 = **16.2**
8. 1.04 + 2.07 = **3.11**
9. 86.7 + 5.2 + 8.4 = **100.3**
10. 42.65 + 67.23 + 12.12 = **122**

11. 10.3 + 7.4 = **17.7**
12. 24.7 + 32.6 = **57.3**
13. 16.52 + 13.63 = **30.15**
14. 9.1 + 12.5 + 19.4 = **41**
15. 492.6 + 382.3 + 225.7 = **1,100.6**

16. 1.5 + 1.5 = **3.0**
17. 20.5 + 32.3 = **52.8**
18. 14.87 + 56.09 = **70.96**
19. 40.08 + 60.27 + 50.33 = **150.68**
20. 4.008 + 1.318 + 0.056 = **5.382**

74   CD-104322 • © Carson-Dellosa

Page 75

Name _____   Date _____

Adding Decimals

Total Problems: 16
Problems Correct: _____

Solve each problem.

1. 2.34 + 0.02 + 1.65 = **4.01**
2. 543.7 + 3.42 + 0.06 = **547.18**
3. 72.56 + 12.38 + 0.07 = **85.01**
4. 22.87 + 45.7 + 1.26 = **69.83**

5. 987.5 + 4.1 + 30.2 = **1,021.8**
6. 2.14 + 0.007 + 72.4 = **74.547**
7. 1.70 + 23.75 + 0.605 = **26.055**
8. 86.15 + 0.07 + 5.72 = **91.94**

9. 5.1 + 7.53 + 87.4 = **100.03**
10. 0.2 + 1.2 + 0.12 = **1.52**
11. 1.45 + 20.03 + 0.17 = **21.65**
12. 4.5 + 5.4 + 12.67 = **22.57**

13. 42.7 + 0.03 + 1.7 = **44.43**
14. 87.5 + 1.2 + 591.35 = **680.05**
15. 0.725 + 1.33 + 12 = **14.055**
16. 42 + 0.543 + 7.8 = **50.343**

CD-104322 • © Carson-Dellosa   75

Name _____ Date _____

Subtracting Decimals

Total Problems: **20**
Problems Correct: _____

Solve each problem.

1. 0.8
− 0.4
0.4

2. 0.47
− 0.21
0.26

3. 0.753
− 0.211
0.542

4. 4.6
− 2.1
2.5

5. 42.53
− 0.25
42.28

6. 0.9
− 0.5
0.4

7. 0.53
− 0.27
0.26

8. 0.867
− 0.501
0.366

9. 5.6
− 0.2
5.4

10. 87.54
− 6.25
81.29

11. 0.3
− 0.1
0.2

12. 0.37
− 0.15
0.22

13. 0.467
− 0.338
0.129

14. 37.6
− 0.7
36.9

15. 95.43
− 16.07
79.36

16. 0.5
− 0.2
0.3

17. 0.42
− 0.12
0.3

18. 0.575
− 0.104
0.471

19. 25.06
− 3.72
21.34

20. 53.27
− 5.42
47.85

76   CD-104322 • © Carson-Dellosa

Name _____ Date _____

Subtracting Decimals

Total Problems: **16**
Problems Correct: _____

Solve each problem.

1. 19.867
− 1.07
18.797

2. 4.52
− 0.4
4.12

3. 6.254
− 3.01
3.244

4. 23.154
− 3.08
20.074

5. 0.7
− 0.506
0.194

6. 20.342
− 0.37
19.972

7. 756.83
− 22.5
734.33

8. 38.7
− 5.21
33.49

9. 1.428
− 1.2
0.228

10. 71.34
− 2.672
68.668

11. 31.1
− 3.052
28.048

12. 0.65
− 0.224
0.426

13. 2.3
− 1.437
0.863

14. 32.456
− 1.2
31.256

15. 81.384
− 2.777
78.607

16. 24.75
− 6.243
18.507

CD-104322 • © Carson-Dellosa   77

Name _____ Date _____

Multiplying Decimals

Total Problems: **20**
Problems Correct: _____

Solve each problem. Round to the nearest thousandth
when necessary.

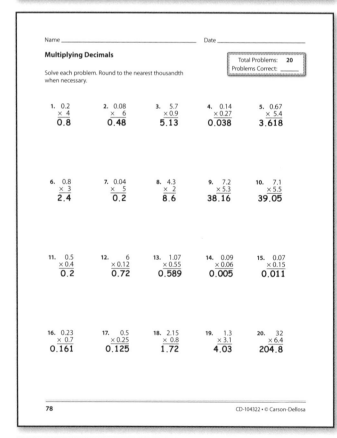

1. 0.2
× 4
0.8

2. 0.08
× 6
0.48

3. 5.7
× 0.9
5.13

4. 0.14
× 0.27
0.038

5. 0.67
× 5.4
3.618

6. 0.8
× 3
2.4

7. 0.04
× 5
0.2

8. 4.3
× 2
8.6

9. 7.2
× 5.3
38.16

10. 7.1
× 5.5
39.05

11. 0.5
× 0.4
0.2

12. 6
× 0.12
0.72

13. 1.07
× 0.55
0.589

14. 0.09
× 0.06
0.005

15. 0.07
× 0.15
0.011

16. 0.23
× 0.7
0.161

17. 0.5
× 0.25
0.125

18. 2.15
× 0.8
1.72

19. 1.3
× 3.1
4.03

20. 32
× 6.4
204.8

78   CD-104322 • © Carson-Dellosa

Name _____ Date _____

Multiplying Decimals

Total Problems: **16**
Problems Correct: _____

Solve each problem. Round to the nearest thousandth
when necessary.

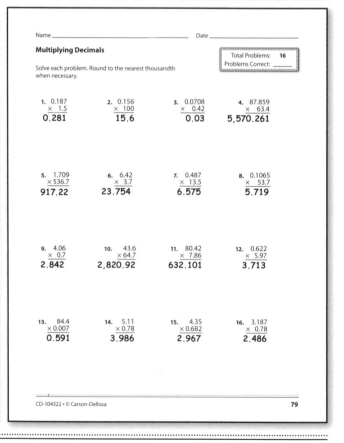

1. 0.187
× 1.5
0.281

2. 0.156
× 100
15.6

3. 0.0708
× 0.42
0.03

4. 87.859
× 63.4
5,570.261

5. 1.709
× 536.7
917.22

6. 6.42
× 3.7
23.754

7. 0.487
× 13.5
6.575

8. 0.1065
× 53.7
5.719

9. 4.06
× 0.7
2.842

10. 43.6
× 64.7
2,820.92

11. 80.42
× 7.86
632.101

12. 0.622
× 5.97
3.713

13. 84.4
× 0.007
0.591

14. 5.11
× 0.78
3.986

15. 4.35
× 0.682
2.967

16. 3.187
× 0.78
2.486

CD-104322 • © Carson-Dellosa   79

Dividing Decimals

Name _____ Date _____

Total Problems: **20**
Problems Correct: _____

Solve each problem.

1. $9\overline{)2.7}$ = **0.3**
2. $7\overline{)2.1}$ = **0.3**
3. $4\overline{)0.16}$ = **0.04**
4. $0.8\overline{)56}$ = **70**

5. $6\overline{)3.6}$ = **0.6**
6. $8\overline{)0.64}$ = **0.08**
7. $9\overline{)0.27}$ = **0.03**
8. $0.07\overline{)2.1}$ = **30**

9. $3\overline{)2.7}$ = **0.9**
10. $6\overline{)0.30}$ = **0.05**
11. $0.04\overline{)28}$ = **700**
12. $0.9\overline{)5.4}$ = **6**

13. $3\overline{)0.18}$ = **0.06**
14. $2\overline{)0.12}$ = **0.06**
15. $0.9\overline{)72}$ = **80**
16. $0.7\overline{)0.35}$ = **0.5**

17. $4\overline{)2.4}$ = **0.6**
18. $5\overline{)2.5}$ = **0.5**
19. $0.04\overline{)36}$ = **900**
20. $0.9\overline{)6.3}$ = **7**

Dividing Decimals

Name _____ Date _____

Total Problems: **16**
Problems Correct: _____

Solve each problem.

1. $4\overline{)9.6}$ = **2.4**
2. $0.5\overline{)12.5}$ = **25**
3. $16\overline{)59.2}$ = **3.7**
4. $1.8\overline{)57.6}$ = **32**

5. $0.15\overline{)75}$ = **500**
6. $1.2\overline{)1.44}$ = **1.2**
7. $1.3\overline{)1.30}$ = **1**
8. $0.09\overline{)0.783}$ = **8.7**

9. $0.2\overline{)1}$ = **5**
10. $3\overline{)0.363}$ = **0.121**
11. $0.27\overline{)648}$ = **2,400**
12. $5.2\overline{)13.52}$ = **2.6**

13. $0.06\overline{)1.20}$ = **20**
14. $5.4\overline{)64.8}$ = **12**
15. $0.5\overline{)10.50}$ = **21**
16. $6.7\overline{)33.5}$ = **5**

Finding Percents

Name _____ Date _____

Total Problems: **25**
Problems Correct: _____

Write each fraction as a percent.

1. $\frac{1}{2}$ = **50%** 2. $\frac{9}{20}$ = **45%** 3. $\frac{3}{4}$ = **75%** 4. $\frac{6}{25}$ = **24%** 5. $\frac{1}{5}$ = **20%**

6. $\frac{2}{5}$ = **40%** 7. $\frac{9}{10}$ = **90%** 8. $\frac{1}{10}$ = **10%** 9. $\frac{1}{4}$ = **25%** 10. $\frac{4}{25}$ = **16%**

Write each percent as a fraction. Write each answer in simplest form.

11. 16% = $\frac{4}{25}$ 12. 35% = $\frac{7}{20}$ 13. 77% = $\frac{77}{100}$ 14. 90% = $\frac{9}{10}$ 15. 25% = $\frac{1}{4}$

16. 33% = $\frac{33}{100}$ 17. 28% = $\frac{7}{25}$ 18. 10% = $\frac{1}{10}$ 19. 5% = $\frac{1}{20}$ 20. 14% = $\frac{7}{50}$

21. 75% = $\frac{3}{4}$ 22. 9% = $\frac{9}{100}$ 23. 40% = $\frac{2}{5}$ 24. 55% = $\frac{11}{20}$ 25. 99% = $\frac{99}{100}$

Finding Percents

Name _____ Date _____

Total Problems: **20**
Problems Correct: _____

Write each decimal as a percent.

1. 0.9 = **90%**
2. 0.007 = **0.7%**

3. 0.52 = **52%**
4. 0.462 = **46.2%**

5. 0.062 = **6.2%**
6. 0.1283 = **12.83%**

7. 0.321 = **32.1%**
8. 0.505 = **50.5%**

9. 0.65 = **65%**
10. 0.3 = **30%**

Write each percent as a decimal.

11. 10% = **0.1**
12. 0.45% = **0.0045**

13. 16.2% = **0.162**
14. 98% = **0.98**

15. 3.5% = **0.035**
16. 2.75% = **0.0275**

17. 8% = **0.08**
18. 10.3% = **0.103**

19. 12.5% = **0.125**
20. 1.75% = **0.0175**

Page 84

Name _____ Date _____

Finding Percents

Total Problems: **15**
Problems Correct: _____

Find the given percent of each number.

1. 10% of 50 = **5**   2. 50% of 48 = **24**   3. 40% of 80 = **32**

4. 60% of 90 = **54**   5. 16% of 64 = **10.24**   6. 70% of 25 = **17.5**

7. 25% of 50 = **12.5**   8. 20% of 100 = **20**   9. 32% of 94 = **30.08**

10. 15% of 45 = **6.75**   11. 85% of 20 = **17**   12. 5% of 57 = **2.85**

13. 97% of 63 = **61.11**   14. 13% of 87 = **11.31**   15. 12% of 32 = **3.84**

84   CD-104322 • © Carson-Dellosa

Page 85

Name _____ Date _____

Fractions, Decimals, and Percents Review

Total Problems: **20**
Problems Correct: _____

Write each fraction as a decimal.

1. $\frac{13}{20}$ = **0.65**   2. $\frac{9}{5}$ = **1.8**   3. $\frac{4}{25}$ = **0.16**   4. $\frac{43}{50}$ = **0.86**

Write each percent as a fraction.

5. 28% = **$\frac{7}{25}$**   6. 64% = **$\frac{16}{25}$**   7. 15% = **$\frac{3}{20}$**   8. 65% = **$\frac{13}{20}$**

Write each decimal as a percent.

9. 0.005 = **0.5%**   10. 0.128 = **12.8%**   11. 0.27 = **27%**   12. 0.6 = **60%**

Change each percent to a decimal.

13. 13.6% = **0.136**   14. 84% = **0.84**   15. 0.37% = **0.0037**   16. 5% = **0.05**

Find the given percent of each number.

17. 6% of 25 = **1.5**   18. 80% of 50 = **40**

19. 9% of 100 = **9**   20. 15% of 30 = **4.5**

CD-104322 • © Carson-Dellosa   85

Page 86

Name _____ Date _____

Fractions, Decimals, and Percents Review

Total Problems: **10**
Problems Correct: _____

Complete the chart. Round to the nearest thousandth when necessary.

	Fraction	Decimal	Percentage
1.	$\frac{17}{100}$	0.17	17%
2.	$\frac{1}{2}$	0.5	50%
3.	$\frac{13}{17}$	0.765	76.5%
4.	$\frac{19}{20}$	0.95	95%
5.	$\frac{3}{4}$	0.75	75%
6.	$\frac{1}{8}$	0.125	12.5%
7.	$\frac{1}{6}$	0.167	16.7%
8.	$\frac{1}{200}$	0.005	0.5%
9.	$\frac{3}{10}$	0.3	30%
10.	$\frac{9}{20}$	0.45	45%

86   CD-104322 • © Carson-Dellosa

Page 87

Name _____ Date _____

Finding the Perimeter of a Polygon

Total Problems: **6**
Problems Correct: _____

Find the perimeter of each figure.

1. Perimeter = **12.5 mi.**

2.5 mi. 2.5 mi. 4.5 mi. 3 mi.

2. Perimeter = **12.8 m**

5.4 m 1 m 1 m 5.4 m

3. Perimeter = **17 in.**

6 in. 4 in. 7 in.

4. Perimeter = **20 yd.**

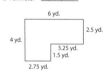
6 yd. 2.5 yd. 4 yd. 3.25 yd. 1.5 yd. 2.75 yd.

5. Perimeter = **13.8 km**

3 km 2.7 km 2.7 km 2.7 km 2.7 km

6. Perimeter = **36 cm**

9 cm 9 cm 9 cm 9 cm

CD-104322 • © Carson-Dellosa   87

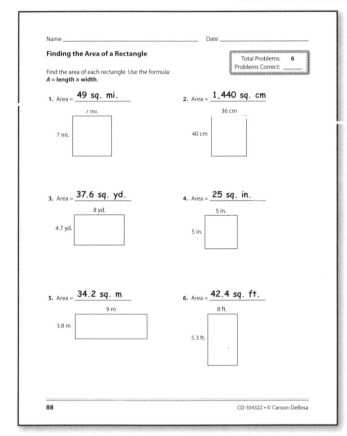

Name _____ Date _____

Finding the Area of a Rectangle

Total Problems: 6
Problems Correct: _____

Find the area of each rectangle. Use the formula:
A = length × width.

1. Area = **49 sq. mi.**
7 mi.
7 mi.

2. Area = **1,440 sq. cm**
36 cm
40 cm

3. Area = **37.6 sq. yd.**
8 yd.
4.7 yd.

4. Area = **25 sq. in.**
5 in.
5 in.

5. Area = **34.2 sq. m**
9 m
3.8 m

6. Area = **42.4 sq. ft.**
8 ft.
5.3 ft.

88   CD-104322 • © Carson-Dellosa

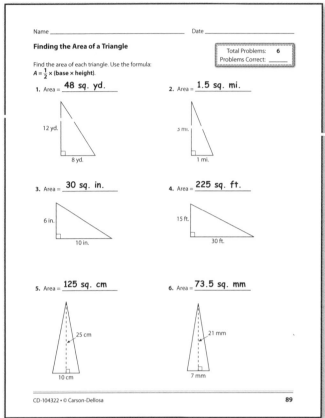

Name _____ Date _____

Finding the Area of a Triangle

Total Problems: 6
Problems Correct: _____

Find the area of each triangle. Use the formula:
$A = \frac{1}{2} \times$ (base × height).

1. Area = **48 sq. yd.**
12 yd.
8 yd.

2. Area = **1.5 sq. mi.**
3 mi.
1 mi.

3. Area = **30 sq. in.**
6 in.
10 in.

4. Area = **225 sq. ft.**
15 ft.
30 ft.

5. Area = **125 sq. cm**
25 cm
10 cm

6. Area = **73.5 sq. mm**
21 mm
7 mm

CD-104322 • © Carson-Dellosa   89

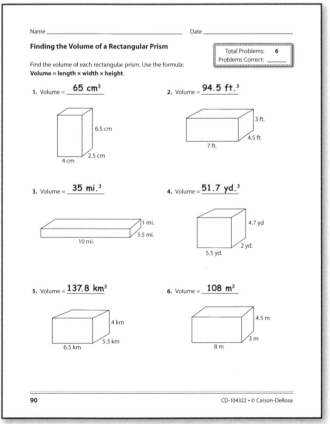

Name _____ Date _____

Finding the Volume of a Rectangular Prism

Total Problems: 6
Problems Correct: _____

Find the volume of each rectangular prism. Use the formula:
Volume = length × width × height.

1. Volume = **65 cm³**
6.5 cm
2.5 cm
4 cm

2. Volume = **94.5 ft.³**
3 ft.
4.5 ft.
7 ft.

3. Volume = **35 mi.³**
1 mi.
3.5 mi.
10 mi.

4. Volume = **51.7 yd.³**
4.7 yd
2 yd.
5.5 yd.

5. Volume = **137.8 km³**
4 km
5.3 km
6.5 km

6. Volume = **108 m³**
4.5 m
3 m
8 m

90   CD-104322 • © Carson-Dellosa

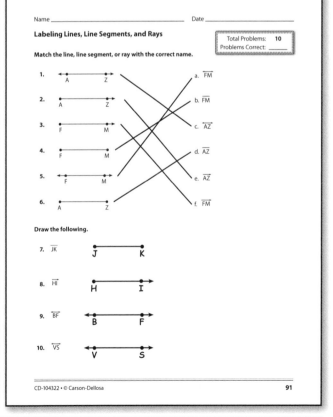

Name _____ Date _____

Labeling Lines, Line Segments, and Rays

Total Problems: 10
Problems Correct: _____

Match the line, line segment, or ray with the correct name.

1.   A   Z   a. $\overline{FM}$

2.   A   Z   b. $\overline{FM}$

3.   F   M   c. $\overline{AZ}$

4.   F   M   d. $\overline{AZ}$

5.   F   M   e. $\overline{AZ}$

6.   A   Z   f. $\overline{FM}$

Draw the following.

7. $\overline{JK}$
J   K

8. $\overrightarrow{HI}$
H   I

9. $\overleftrightarrow{BF}$
B   F

10. $\overleftrightarrow{VS}$
V   S

CD-104322 • © Carson-Dellosa   91

Answer Key

Name _____ Date _____

Naming and Measuring Angles

Total Problems:	5
Problems Correct:	___

Name the angle and use a protractor to measure it.

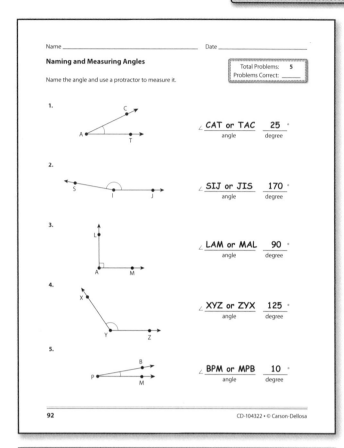

1.

∠ _CAT or TAC_ _25_ °
    angle   degree

2.

∠ _SIJ or JIS_ _170_ °
    angle   degree

3.

∠ _LAM or MAL_ _90_ °
    angle   degree

4.

∠ _XYZ or ZYX_ _125_ °
    angle   degree

5.

∠ _BPM or MPB_ _10_ °
    angle   degree

92   CD-104322 • © Carson-Dellosa

Name _____ Date _____

Finding the Circumference of a Circle

Total Problems:	6
Problems Correct:	___

Find the circumference of each circle. Use the formula:
Circumference = π × diameter OR Circumference = π × 2 × radius.
Remember, **π = 3.14**.

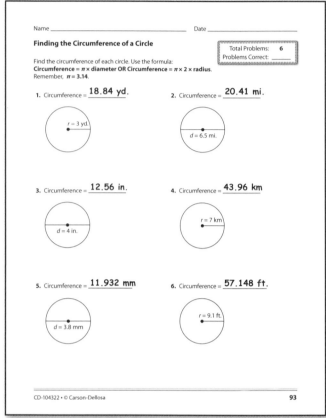

1. Circumference = _18.84 yd._

2. Circumference = _20.41 mi._

3. Circumference = _12.56 in._

4. Circumference = _43.96 km_

5. Circumference = _11.932 mm_

6. Circumference = _57.148 ft._

CD-104322 • © Carson-Dellosa   93

Name _____ Date _____

Labeling Bar and Circle Graphs

Total Problems:	2
Problems Correct:	___

1. Use the information below to make a bar graph. First, name the graph. Next, name and label the x-axis and y-axis. Finally, graph the data.

Number of pieces of trash picked up on Environment Day	
1st grade	26
2nd grade	21
3rd grade	25
4th grade	17
5th grade	22
6th grade	29

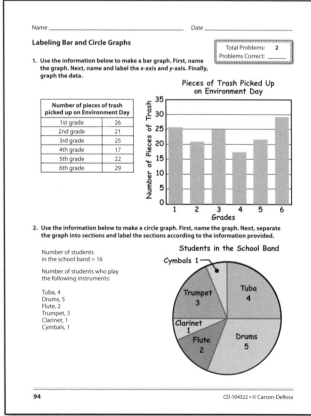

2. Use the information below to make a circle graph. First, name the graph. Next, separate the graph into sections and label the sections according to the information provided.

Number of students in the school band = 16

Number of students who play the following instruments:

Tuba, 4
Drums, 5
Flute, 2
Trumpet, 3
Clarinet, 1
Cymbals, 1

94   CD-104322 • © Carson-Dellosa

Name _____ Date _____

Labeling Line Graphs

Total Problems:	2
Problems Correct:	___

1. Use the information below to make a line graph. First, name the graph. Next, name and label the x-axis and the y-axis. Finally, plot the data.

Number of times that John went to the zoo last year	
January	1
February	3
March	2
April	4
May	2
June	5
July	7
August	4
September	1
October	4
November	3
December	2

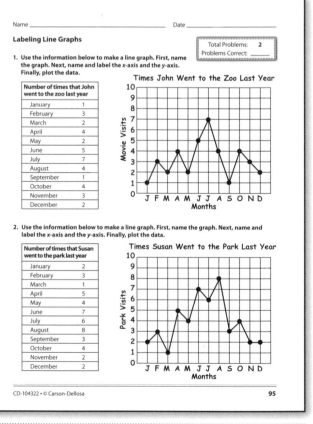

2. Use the information below to make a line graph. First, name the graph. Next, name and label the x-axis and the y-axis. Finally, plot the data.

Number of times that Susan went to the park last year	
January	2
February	3
March	1
April	5
May	4
June	7
July	6
August	8
September	3
October	4
November	2
December	2

CD-104322 • © Carson-Dellosa   95

Name _____ Date _____

Graphing Coordinates

Graph each pair of coordinates.

Total Problems: **12**
Problems Correct: _____

1. (3, 4)
2. (7, 8)
3. (5, 1)
4. (3, 7)
5. (8, 2)
6. (6, 10)

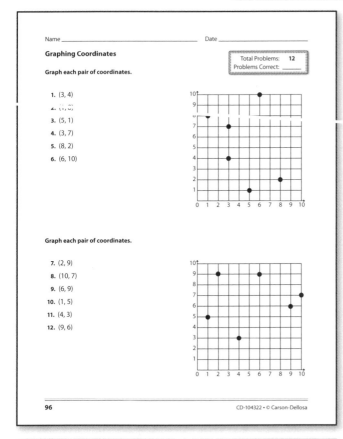

Graph each pair of coordinates.

7. (2, 9)
8. (10, 7)
9. (6, 9)
10. (1, 5)
11. (4, 3)
12. (9, 6)

Name _____ Date _____

Graphing Coordinates

Graph each pair of coordinates.

Total Problems: **12**
Problems Correct: _____

1. (3, 5)
2. (7, 8)
3. (1, 3)
4. (6, 10)
5. (9, 4)
6. (8, 1)

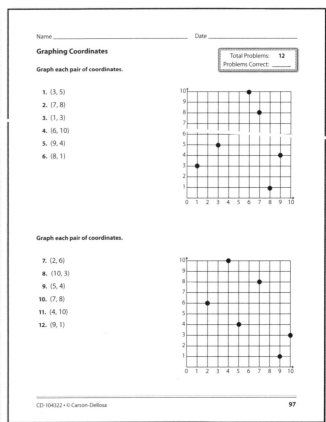

Graph each pair of coordinates.

7. (2, 6)
8. (10, 3)
9. (5, 4)
10. (7, 8)
11. (4, 10)
12. (9, 1)

Name _____ Date _____

Graphing Coordinates

Graph each pair of coordinates.

Total Problems: **12**
Problems Correct: _____

1. (6, 5)
2. (1, 7)
3. (10, 9)
4. (8, 3)
5. (5, 8)
6. (7, 2)

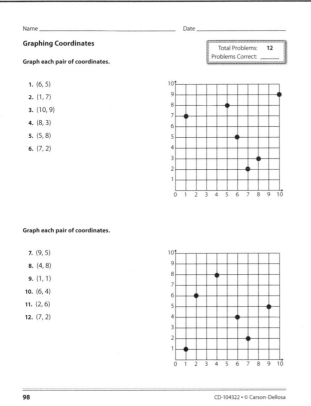

Graph each pair of coordinates.

7. (9, 5)
8. (4, 8)
9. (1, 1)
10. (6, 4)
11. (2, 6)
12. (7, 2)

Name _____ Date _____

Number Patterns

Total Problems: **14**
Problems Correct: _____

Find the next three numbers in each number pattern.

1. 5, 8, 11, 14, 17, __20__, __21__, __24__

2. 91, 86, 81, 76, 71, __66__, __61__, __56__

3. 100, 92, 84, 76, 68, __60__, __52__, __44__

4. 10, 20, 25, 35, 40, __50__, __55__, __65__

5. 72, 69, 66, 63, 60, __57__, __54__, __51__

6. 317, 402, 487, 572, __657__, __742__, __827__

7. 5, 11, 23, 47, 95, __191__, __383__, __767__

8. 244, 226, 208, 190, __172__, __154__, __136__

9. 1, 4, 9, 16, 25, __36__, __49__, __64__

10. 1, 2, 4, 8, 16, __32__, __64__, __128__

11. 53, 54, 56, 59, 63, __68__, __74__, __81__

12. 30, 34, 40, 48, 58, __70__, __84__, __100__

13. 11, 16, 14, 19, 17, __22__, __20__, __25__

14. 19, 34, 49, 64, 79, __94__, __109__, __124__

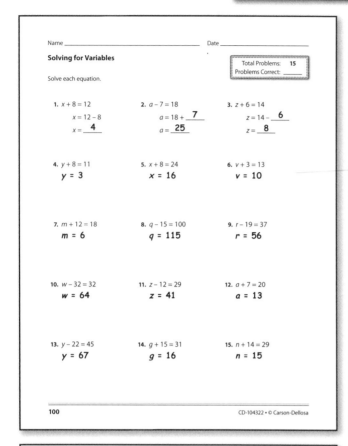

Name _____ Date _____

Solving for Variables

Total Problems:	15
Problems Correct:	_____

Solve each equation.

1. $x + 8 = 12$
$x = 12 - 8$
$x = \underline{4}$

2. $a - 7 = 18$
$a = 18 + \underline{7}$
$a = \underline{25}$

3. $z + 6 = 14$
$z = 14 - \underline{6}$
$z = \underline{8}$

4. $y + 8 = 11$
$y = 3$

5. $x + 8 = 24$
$x = 16$

6. $v + 3 = 13$
$v = 10$

7. $m + 12 = 18$
$m = 6$

8. $q - 15 = 100$
$q = 115$

9. $r - 19 = 37$
$r = 56$

10. $w - 32 = 32$
$w = 64$

11. $z - 12 = 29$
$z = 41$

12. $a + 7 = 20$
$a = 13$

13. $y - 22 = 45$
$y = 67$

14. $g + 15 = 31$
$g = 16$

15. $n + 14 = 29$
$n = 15$

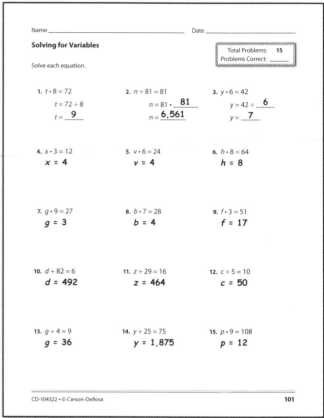

Name _____ Date _____

Solving for Variables

Total Problems:	15
Problems Correct:	_____

Solve each equation.

1. $t \cdot 8 = 72$
$t = 72 \div 8$
$t = \underline{9}$

2. $n \div 81 = 81$
$n = 81 \cdot \underline{81}$
$n = \underline{6{,}561}$

3. $y \cdot 6 = 42$
$y = 42 \div \underline{6}$
$y = \underline{7}$

4. $x \cdot 3 = 12$
$x = 4$

5. $v \cdot 6 = 24$
$v = 4$

6. $h \cdot 8 = 64$
$h = 8$

7. $g \cdot 9 = 27$
$g = 3$

8. $b \cdot 7 = 28$
$b = 4$

9. $f \cdot 3 = 51$
$f = 17$

10. $d \div 82 = 6$
$d = 492$

11. $z \div 29 = 16$
$z = 464$

12. $c \div 5 = 10$
$c = 50$

13. $g \div 4 = 9$
$g = 36$

14. $y \div 25 = 75$
$y = 1{,}875$

15. $p \cdot 9 = 108$
$p = 12$

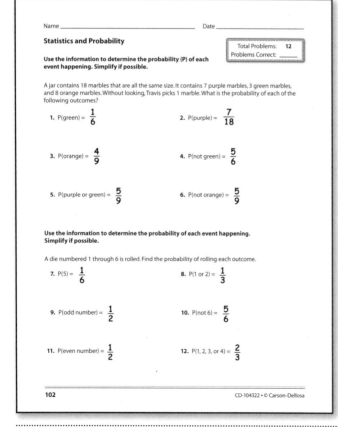

Name _____ Date _____

Statistics and Probability

Total Problems:	12
Problems Correct:	_____

Use the information to determine the probability (P) of each event happening. Simplify if possible.

A jar contains 18 marbles that are all the same size. It contains 7 purple marbles, 3 green marbles, and 8 orange marbles. Without looking, Travis picks 1 marble. What is the probability of each of the following outcomes?

1. P(green) = $\frac{1}{6}$

2. P(purple) = $\frac{7}{18}$

3. P(orange) = $\frac{4}{9}$

4. P(not green) = $\frac{5}{6}$

5. P(purple or green) = $\frac{5}{9}$

6. P(not orange) = $\frac{5}{9}$

Use the information to determine the probability of each event happening. Simplify if possible.

A die numbered 1 through 6 is rolled. Find the probability of rolling each outcome.

7. P(5) = $\frac{1}{6}$

8. P(1 or 2) = $\frac{1}{3}$

9. P(odd number) = $\frac{1}{2}$

10. P(not 6) = $\frac{5}{6}$

11. P(even number) = $\frac{1}{2}$

12. P(1, 2, 3, or 4) = $\frac{2}{3}$

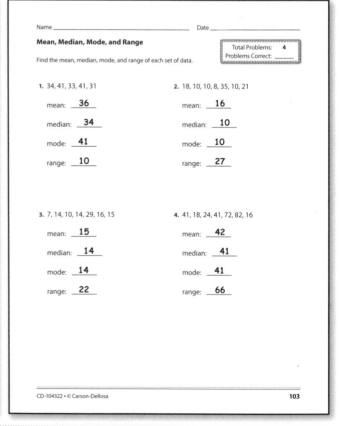

Name _____ Date _____

Mean, Median, Mode, and Range

Total Problems:	4
Problems Correct:	_____

Find the mean, median, mode, and range of each set of data.

1. 34, 41, 33, 41, 31

mean: $\underline{36}$

median: $\underline{34}$

mode: $\underline{41}$

range: $\underline{10}$

2. 18, 10, 10, 8, 35, 10, 21

mean: $\underline{16}$

median: $\underline{10}$

mode: $\underline{10}$

range: $\underline{27}$

3. 7, 14, 10, 14, 29, 16, 15

mean: $\underline{15}$

median: $\underline{14}$

mode: $\underline{14}$

range: $\underline{22}$

4. 41, 18, 24, 41, 72, 82, 16

mean: $\underline{42}$

median: $\underline{41}$

mode: $\underline{41}$

range: $\underline{66}$

Congratulations!

receives this award for

_____

_____

Signed _____

Date _____

© Carson-Dellosa

Solve.

$$522 + 326$$

Solve.

$$52{,}554 + 214$$

Solve.

$$251 + 854 + 741$$

Solve.

$$2{,}563 + 523 + 41$$

© CD

Solve.

$$111 - 85$$

Solve.

$$258 - 133$$

Solve.

$$459 - 28$$

Solve.

$$21{,}359 - 15{,}886$$

© CD

Solve.

$$212 \times 12$$

Solve.

$$5{,}627 \times 42$$

Solve.

$$159 \times 36$$

Solve.

$$658 \times 986$$

© CD

Solve.

$$120 \overline{)3{,}600}$$

Solve.

$$5 \overline{)655}$$

Solve.

$$25 \overline{)3{,}455}$$

Solve.

$$6 \overline{)5{,}470}$$

© CD

3,127	1,846	52,768	848
5,473	431	125	26
648,788	5,724	236,334	2,544
911 r4	138 r5	131	30

Change to a mixed number.

$$\frac{45}{10}$$

© CD

Change to a mixed number.

$$\frac{62}{11}$$

© CD

Change to a mixed number.

$$\frac{20}{17}$$

© CD

Change to a mixed number.

$$\frac{125}{41}$$

© CD

Change to an improper fraction.

$$7\frac{1}{4}$$

© CD

Change to an improper fraction.

$$15\frac{1}{2}$$

© CD

Find the equivalent.

$$\frac{6}{15} = \frac{}{75}$$

© CD

Find the equivalent.

$$\frac{3}{8} = \frac{}{56}$$

© CD

Find the equivalent.

$$\frac{5}{25} = \frac{}{50}$$

© CD

Find the equivalent.

$$\frac{5}{8} = \frac{}{48}$$

© CD

Find the equivalent.

$$\frac{6}{20} = \frac{}{100}$$

© CD

Find the equivalent.

$$\frac{4}{9} = \frac{}{63}$$

© CD

Solve.

$$\frac{2}{9} \times \frac{2}{9} =$$

© CD

Solve.

$$\frac{1}{4} \times \frac{7}{8} =$$

© CD

Solve.

$$2 \times \frac{5}{8} =$$

© CD

Solve.

$$4 \times \frac{4}{5} =$$

© CD

$3\frac{2}{41}$

$3\frac{1}{5}$

21

28

$1\frac{3}{17}$

$1\frac{1}{4}$

30

30

$5\frac{7}{11}$

$\frac{31}{2}$

30

$\frac{7}{32}$

30

$4\frac{1}{2}$

$\frac{29}{4}$

10

$\frac{4}{81}$

© CD

Solve.

$$\frac{3}{7} \times \frac{1}{10} =$$

© CD

Change to simplest form.

$$\frac{25}{100}$$

© CD

Change to simplest form.

$$\frac{7}{56}$$

© CD

Fill in the circle with <, >, or =.

$$\frac{8}{20} \bigcirc \frac{2}{5}$$

© CD

Solve.

$$\frac{1}{8} \times \frac{1}{7} =$$

© CD

Change to simplest form.

$$\frac{2}{26}$$

© CD

Change to simplest form.

$$\frac{15}{90}$$

© CD

Fill in the circle with <, >, or =.

$$\frac{6}{9} \bigcirc \frac{1}{3}$$

© CD

Solve.

$$2\frac{6}{11} \times 5\frac{1}{2} =$$

© CD

Change to simplest form.

$$\frac{14}{28}$$

© CD

Change to simplest form.

$$\frac{15}{675}$$

© CD

Fill in the circle with <, >, or =.

$$\frac{3}{5} \bigcirc \frac{2}{3}$$

© CD

Solve.

$$3\frac{1}{3} \times 1\frac{7}{9} =$$

© CD

Change to simplest form.

$$\frac{3}{21}$$

© CD

Change to simplest form.

$$\frac{10}{55}$$

© CD

Fill in the circle with <, >, or =.

$$\frac{13}{20} \bigcirc \frac{45}{80}$$

© CD

$5\frac{25}{27}$ 14 $\frac{1}{56}$ $\frac{3}{70}$

$\frac{1}{7}$ $\frac{1}{2}$ $\frac{1}{13}$ $\frac{1}{4}$

$\frac{2}{11}$ $\frac{1}{45}$ $\frac{1}{6}$ $\frac{1}{8}$

$>$ $<$ $>$ $=$

Solve.

$$\frac{2}{24} + \frac{3}{24}$$

Solve.

$$\frac{1}{6} + \frac{1}{4}$$

Solve.

$$\frac{11}{12} - \frac{1}{12}$$

Solve.

$$8\frac{1}{2} - 8\frac{1}{4}$$

Solve.

$$\frac{2}{7} + \frac{5}{7}$$

Solve.

$$\frac{3}{5} + \frac{4}{7}$$

Solve.

$$3\frac{1}{3} + 11\frac{2}{3}$$

Solve.

$$19 - \frac{1}{2}$$

Solve.

$$5\frac{1}{9} + 7\frac{8}{9}$$

Solve.

$$2\frac{3}{8} + 5\frac{1}{2}$$

Solve.

$$4\frac{1}{2} + 7\frac{3}{10}$$

Solve.

$$8 - \frac{5}{8}$$

Solve.

$$6\frac{2}{3} + 4\frac{2}{3}$$

Solve.

$$4\frac{7}{8} + 6\frac{3}{4}$$

Solve.

$$5\frac{2}{5} + 4\frac{3}{8}$$

Solve.

$$\frac{5}{7} - \frac{2}{9}$$

© CD

$$\frac{5}{24} \qquad 1 \qquad 13 \qquad 11\frac{1}{3}$$

$$\frac{5}{12} \qquad 1\frac{6}{35} \qquad 7\frac{7}{8} \qquad 11\frac{5}{8}$$

$$\frac{5}{6} \qquad 15 \qquad 11\frac{4}{5} \qquad 9\frac{31}{40}$$

$$\frac{1}{4} \qquad 18\frac{1}{2} \qquad 7\frac{3}{8} \qquad \frac{31}{63}$$

Solve.

$$14.6 + 12.18$$

© CD

Solve.

$$44.2 + 445$$

© CD

Solve.

$$0.3 + 0.005$$

© CD

Solve.

$$35.6 + 77.7$$

© CD

Solve.

$$45.4 - 5.4$$

© CD

Solve.

$$34.9 - 13.3$$

© CD

Solve.

$$122.52 - 65.3$$

© CD

Solve.

$$8.5 - 3.2$$

© CD

Solve.

$$15.46 \times 0.4$$

© CD

Solve.

$$5.2 \times 0.16$$

© CD

Solve.

$$41.2 \times 1.1$$

© CD

Solve.

$$47.8 \times 1.23$$

© CD

Solve.

$$6\overline{)2.4}$$

© CD

Solve.

$$8\overline{)0.48}$$

© CD

Solve.

$$0.9\overline{)10.8}$$

© CD

Solve.

$$0.2\overline{)16}$$

© CD

113.3	0.305	489.2	26.78
5.3	57.22	21.6	40
58.794	45.32	0.832	6.184
80	12	0.06	0.4

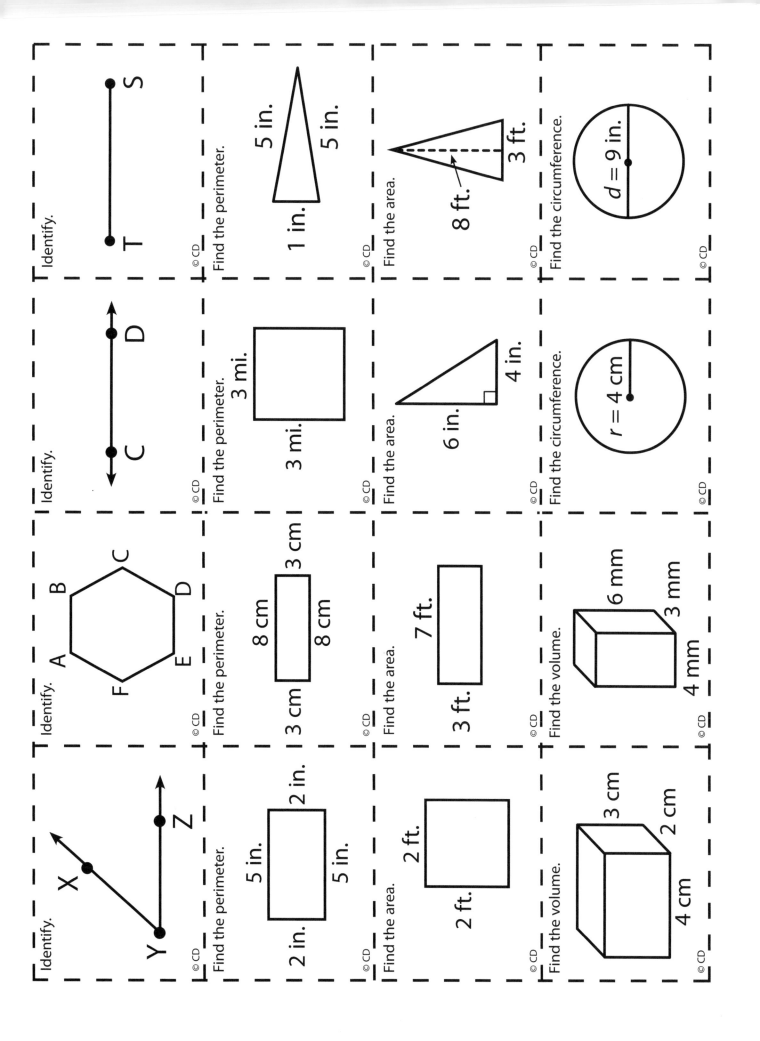

Identify. X Y Z

Identify. A B C D E F

Identify. C D

Identify. T S

Find the perimeter. 5 in. 2 in. 2 in. 5 in.

Find the perimeter. 8 cm 3 cm 3 cm 8 cm

Find the perimeter. 3 mi. 3 mi.

Find the perimeter. 5 in. 5 in. 1 in.

Find the area. 2 ft. 2 ft.

Find the area. 7 ft. 3 ft.

Find the area. 6 in. 4 in.

Find the area. 8 ft. 3 ft.

Find the volume. 4 cm 3 cm 2 cm

Find the volume. 6 mm 3 mm 4 mm

Find the circumference. r = 4 cm

Find the circumference. d = 9 in.

© CD

| Line | Line CD | Hexagon ABCDEF | ∠XYZ |
| Segment TS | | | |

11 in. 12 mi. 22 cm 14 in.

12 sq. ft. 12 sq. in. 21 sq. ft. 4 sq. ft.

28.26 in. 25.12 cm 72 mm³ 24 cm³